Victor M. Grimm, Esq.

Landlord & Tenant Guide to Colorado EVICTIONS

Bradford Publishing Company
Denver, Colorado

PLEASE READ

This book, Landlord and Tenant Guide to Colorado Evictions, is intended to provide general information with regard to the subject matter covered. It is not meant to provide legal opinions or offer advice, nor to serve as a substitute for advice by licensed, legal professionals. It is sold with the understanding that Bradford Publishing Company is not engaged in rendering legal or other professional services.

Bradford Publishing Company and the author do not warrant that the information herein is complete or accurate, and do not assume and hereby disclaim any liability to any person for any loss or damage caused by errors, inaccuracies or omissions, or usage of this book or its forms.

Laws, and interpretations of those laws, change frequently and the subject matter of this book contains important legal consequences. It is the responsibility of the user of this book to know if the information contained in it are applicable to his or her situation, and if necessary, to consult legal, tax or other counsel.

Landlord and Tenant Guide to Colorado Evictions

ISBN 1-883726-03-4

Dedication

This book is dedicated to the memory of my grandfather, Louis Supera, who transformed old boiler rooms into saunas, gangways into colorful entries, and basements into garden apartments. He created affordable housing for the working men and women of Chicago. His sense of creativity, fairness and the importance of affordable shelter for all has greatly inspired this book and my life.

I also wish to acknowledge the invaluable assistance of my wife/Legal Assistant, Denise Grimm, in the drafting, research, revisions and most importantly, moral support in conjunction with this endeavor and my legal pursuits generally.

Table of Contents

Introduction

"Landlord"..."Tenant"..."Eviction"... These terms bring to mind colorful stereotypes of events and characters from our collective consciousness. A "Landlord" is imagined as a slimy-looking man with a pencil moustache, black cape and top hat, leering at the young widow demanding "You must pay the rent!" The archetypal "tenant" takes on one of two forms: (a) the hapless, share-cropper living in poverty conditions working 10 hour days, 7 days a week to pay the wealthy plantation owner the inflated annual rent on his run down shack and square of infertile crop land; or (b) the sadistic societal leach, who after making outrageous demands for special treatment from the landlord (e.g., "The heat must remain at 98.7°," "Fix my leaking faucet, tonight!, even if it is 2:00 a.m.!") fails to pay rent, draws out eviction litigation for six months, leaves the apartment trashed and then goes on to find his next unsuspecting victim. See the 1991 movie, *Pacific Heights* for instance.

Unfortunately, these stereotypes also carry over into much of the legal literature on the subject. There is almost no end to the articles, seminars and books directed at attorneys and real estate professionals focusing on evictions "from the landlord's perspective," i.e., how-to throw the deadbeat out. Less common, but also present, are "Tenants' Rights Advocates" perspectives replete with shining armor and white horses. Many of these writings tend to present a landlord or tenant's attorney in court arguing his respective case, and lose sight of the fact that someone on the other side might be reading the same writings. This manual attempts to be a value-neutral guide for both the landlord and tenant involved in eviction proceedings.

In Colorado there is no such thing as an "Eviction." The legal procedure under which a landlord regains possession of leased premises from a tenant is an action for "Unlawful Detainer." This is a civil court action brought pursuant to the Forcible Entry and Detainer ("FED") Statute (§ 13-40-101 et seq. C.R.S.) enacted by the Colorado State Legislature. The FED Statute also prohibits the forcible recapture of real property and addresses the procedures involving mortgagors and mortgagees, contract purchasers and vendors, trespassers and squatters. These procedures, although similar, are outside the scope of this book and will not be discussed here. The term "eviction" will be used throughout this book because it is less cumbersome and more recognizable than "Action for Unlawful Detainer." It should be noted that many experienced real estate lawyers incorrectly use the term "forcible" or "FED" when referring to unlawful detainer actions. However, it should be kept in mind that none of the courts or legal forms employ the term "eviction."

HOW TO USE THIS GUIDE

For the landlord, this Guide sets out in chronological order, the steps which must be undertaken to legally dispossess a tenant of the leased premises, from the initial default to the sheriff physically removing the tenant. These steps detail the procedures which must be adhered to so as not to violate any of the tenant's legal rights. Scrupulous attention to these procedures not only safeguards the tenant's legal rights, but will also help assure a speedier resolution and reduce the chance that the judge will throw out the landlord's case on a "technicality."

The tenant facing an eviction should not simply skip over the landlord's legal procedures and go on to the defense section. Rather, the tenant should review the landlord's actions carefully in light of the law. An omission by a landlord may, at best, be a complete defense to the eviction action; at worst, it provides material for the tenant to negotiate with the landlord. Additionally, the section on tenant's defenses contains procedure and substantive information on how to oppose an eviction as well as a brief discussion on the other legal actions a tenant may take including security deposit actions. This section should also be helpful to the landlord in understanding what rights Colorado law gives to tenants and what defenses the landlord might face in court.

Certain paragraphs are set in boxes and noted by the symbol **"E.G."** This symbol stands for the Latin phrase, "exempli gratia," which means "for example." These paragraphs highlight particularly illustrative cases, examples or situations.

FORMS

Almost all of the forms used in this book are printed by Bradford Publishing Company, 1743 Wazee Street, Denver, Colorado 80202, (303-292-2500). Blank forms are available from the publisher as well as many local office supply stores. Next to the "Form Checklist" and "How to Fill Out" sections of respective forms, the Form Identification Number is included. A complete list of the Form Titles and Identification Numbers is also included in the Appendix. When ordering these forms, refer to the Identification Number listed in parenthesis (e.g., No. 235 PA). All forms referred to in this book are for county court. County court deals with claims under $10,000.

LEGAL CITATIONS

Legal citations to cases and articles are contained in endnotes. If additional explanation on an issue or support for an argument in court is required, the specific statute, case or article may be obtained through your local law library. Almost every county in Colorado has one that is open to the public. Call your local county clerk of court for the specific location. Citations to statutory law; the Colorado Revised Statutes (**"C.R.S."**) and the Colorado Rules of Civil Procedure (**"C.R.C.P."**) are also contained in the endnotes (e.g., § 13-40-101, C.R.S.). Most of these statutory citations are to the FED Statute which is officially codified as Sections 101 through 123, contained in Article 40 of Title 13 of the C.R.S. The FED Statute and other relevant laws are reproduced in the appendix of this book.

A bibliography of sources relied upon in the preparation of this book is also included in the Appendix. Parties needing further information on a particular subject are strongly urged to refer to these publications.

CAUTION

This Guide is written so as to be comprehensible to non-lawyers. It may also be helpful to new attorneys and those who are in general practice and rarely represent parties in evictions. THIS BOOK SHOULD NOT BE VIEWED AS A SUBSTITUTE TO PROFESSIONAL CONSULTATION OR REPRESENTATION IN AN EVICTION, BUT RATHER AS A SUPPLEMENT. Although a typical eviction is fairly straightforward, each case has its own unique set of facts which may or may not be relevant to the case. A book such as this written on general procedures cannot, of course, address all contingencies and should not be expected to do so. The Guide attempts to give a good overview of the complete eviction process but it is not an exhaustive treatise on the subject. Many cases, explanations and issues have been omitted to keep this book streamlined. Thus, if you are facing a situation beyond the scope of this Guide, please seek professional counsel at once. The law as it exists today is not necessarily the law of tomorrow. New cases and statutes are constantly coming down, expanding, contracting or eliminating rights and issues.

It should be noted that this book does not address local municipal laws which effect landlord/tenant relations (e.g. an ordinance exists in the City of Boulder requiring interest to be paid on security deposits). Nor does this book deal with federal law implications or rules (e.g. eviction of "Chapter 8" subsidized tenants). Finally, this book does not deal with mobile home park leases or evictions (see Mobile Home Park Act, § 38-12-200.1 et seq., C.R.S.) which are quite different from evictions of a residential apartment or house tenant.

I. Overview of Eviction Procedure

A. BASIC STEPS IN THE EVICTION PROCESS

The eviction process can be broken down into three fundamental steps: (1) pre-litigation notice; (2) litigation; and (3) post-litigation execution.

1. Pre-Litigation Notice

Absent certain clearly delineated exceptions, all eviction cases must be preceded by a notice from the landlord served upon the tenant. Depending upon the situation, this may be: (a) DEMAND FOR COMPLIANCE or POSSESSION (also known as a 3 Day Notice); (b) NOTICE TO VACATE (also known as a 10 Day Notice); (c) NOTICE TO QUIT (Repeat Violation of Covenant); (d) NOTICE TO QUIT (Substantial Violation); and/or (e) Notice as set forth in the lease. This Notice basically serves to give the tenant notice that a problem exists and may (depending on the situation) give the tenant options relating to the tenancy.

2. Litigation

After the proper notice is given, the formal court proceedings are commenced by the filing and serving of a COMPLAINT and SUMMONS. The complaint is the landlord's request to the court for relief in recovering possession and/or damages from the tenant. The summons requires the tenant to participate in court proceedings or face a default judgment. The filing of a complaint opens a file with the court which is assigned a CIVIL ACTION NUMBER. After being served with the complaint, the tenant is given until a specified time, the RETURN DATE, to file an ANSWER. The answer sets forth the tenant's response to the complaint and summons, including defenses and counterclaims against the landlord. A trial date is then set. At the trial, the court hears the landlord's and tenant's cases and renders a decision or JUDGMENT.

3. POST-LITIGATION EXECUTION

If the trial results in a judgment against the tenant for possession of the leased premises, a WRIT OF RESTITUTION will be issued after 48 hours. This writ orders the sheriff to remove the tenant and the tenant's possessions from the premises. The sheriff will then physically remove the tenant and possessions (or supervise removal by a third party) if the tenant does not cooperate by leaving voluntarily.

B. APPROXIMATE TIME FRAME

Contrary to the popular perception, eviction proceedings are relatively expeditious. From pre-litigation notice through recovery of possession, an eviction can taken anywhere from 3 days to 3 months, depending upon numerous factors. If an appeal occurs, years can be added. However, the average contested eviction takes approximately three to ten weeks. The following flowchart is illustrative of the time periods involved.

C. EVICTION FLOWCHART

PRE-LITIGATION

1. Default/End of Lease Term/Periodic Tenancy Termination Period
(1 day – unknown)

2. Pre-Litigation Notice [Demand for Compliance or Possession/Notice to Quit]
(3 days – 10 days; longer if provided in lease or periodic tenancy)

3. *a)* Tenant fails to comply
(1 day – unknown)

b) Tenant complies within Notice Period
(case over)

c) Notice to Quit period lapses
(proceed with case)

LITIGATION

4. Complaint filed with court, Summons issued, placed with sheriff or third party for service
1 – 5 days

5. *a)* Tenant served
5-9 days

b) Tenant not served
(Diligent effort made)
(1 day – unknown)

Post notice upon premises *(Go to **6**)*
[Jurisdiction for Possession only]
[Alias Summons issued] *(Go to **4**)*

6. Return Date

a) Tenant files Answer (0-5 days)

Additional time if good cause, and/or bond posted, or court docket full

b) Tenant doesn't file Answer (0-4 days)

Default Order
*(Go to **8** a)*

7. Trial

POST-LITIGATION EXECUTION

8. *a)* Tenant loses (2 days)

b) Tenant wins (case over)

9. Writ of Restitution issued
(2-14 days)
[Certain holidays may add more time]
[Some counties may send Notice of Pending Eviction or telephone prior to sending sheriff]

10. Sheriff dispossesses tenant

Note: Appeal to higher court if the tenant loses is not considered in this chart.

D. APPROXIMATE COST

Eviction actions may be brought either in the county court or the district court. Different filing fees apply to the different courts. Cases involving amounts under $10,000.00, which include almost all eviction actions, are brought in the county court. The parameters of the fees are set by the state law. (See § 13-32-101, et seq. C.R.S., clerk fees; § 30-1-104, et seq. C.R.S., sheriff fees.) However, counties have some variance in fees, especially sheriff fees. The fees tend to change periodically so it is advisable to check with your county's clerk of court and sheriff for specific prices. The current fees for county court are set forth below.

Clerk		
Complaint filing fee:	$31.00	
Answer (no Counterclaim):	26.00	
Answer (with Counterclaim):	31.00	
Sheriff		
Service of Process:	$15.00	(may be less, not more) + mileage fees ($.12 per mile or more)
Writ of Restitution:	15.00-35.00	plus actual transportation costs

E. NEGOTIATION AND MEDITATION

Extra-judicial negotiation/mediation and settlement of landlord/tenant disputes is almost always preferable to court proceedings and judgments. This is true for numerous reasons:

1. Parties reaching resolution "on their own" tend to be more cooperative in carrying out their respective resolution (e.g. vacation of premises, payment of rent).
2. The procedure of negotiation or mediation is less costly.
3. Negotiation or mediation is usually more expeditious.

4. Parties reaching a negotiated or mediated settlement "feel better" about themselves, each other, and the resolution process than those who must go through the legal system.
5. Negotiating and mediating "minor" disputes leaves the overburdened court system available to resolve "major" disputes.
6. If mediation or negotiation fails, the parties can pursue their legal remedies and the judge will at least know the parties attempted to work it out before running to the courthouse.
7. Some judges will actually *require* that certain disputes be taken to mediation before allowing the case to proceed.

Numerous mediation programs exist throughout Colorado. Some programs have special mediators who handle nothing other than landlord/tenant disputes. A partial list of mediation programs is contained in Appendix E. If an agreement is reached, it should always be memorialized in writing.[1]

F. WRITTEN LEASES

One aspect of landlord/tenant law which cannot be emphasized enough is the importance and priority of the lease. In almost all situations where there is a conflict between the common law and lease provisions, the lease will control. Therefore, before the landlord or tenant contemplates any type of action, THE LEASE SHOULD BE REVIEWED FOR APPLICABLE PROVISIONS. This is particularly important in regard to notice, security deposit and rental liability issues.

G. SELF-HELP/ABANDONMENT/ LANDLORD'S LIEN

One of the most common questions to arise when a landlord/tenant problem occurs is whether self-help is available or if a landlord must resort to the court for remedies. Two other related questions are: (1) What can a landlord do if a tenant abandons the premises? and (2) Can a landlord take a tenant's personal property through a "Landlord's Lien"? The answers to all these questions are inextricably tied to both factual and legal issues.

1. Self-Help

One sure way for a landlord to turn the bad situation of a defaulting tenant into a worse situation is to undertake a self-help remedy without carefully and thoroughly considering the lease, the law and the facts involved in the particular case. In landlord/tenant disputes self-help is the practice of "taking the law into your own hands" and attempting to enforce a lease without court assistance. The case reports are filled with horror stories of landlords who wrongfully entered the leased premises and were held liable for such wrongful acts as trespass, conversion and outrageous conduct.[2] Several of these cases resulted in large punitive damages being assessed against the landlord.[3]

Many leases contain provisions allowing the landlord to undertake self-help remedies.[4] However, commentators and case law are divided as to whether such self-help is permissible under Colorado law.[5] Although an interesting and convincing theoretical argument can be made for the continued viability of self-help, the practical reality is that the time gained or court costs saved by exercising self-help are much outweighed by the severe penalties a landlord faces for a wrongful eviction. THUS, SELF-HELP SHOULD BE AVOIDED AND NEVER BE TRIED WITHOUT CONSULTING AN ATTORNEY.

2. Abandonment

Many leases permit re-entry of leased premises upon abandonment without resort to a court order.[6] Case law is clear that this type of self-help is legal.[7] However, the requisite facts for the establishment of an abandonment are very case-sensitive.[8] If an abandonment is not established, the landlord may once again be held liable for various torts and be subjected to severe penalties.[9]

Case law sets forth two requirements which must be met before an abandonment exists:

An act of abandonment; and

An intent to relinquish the premises.[10]

The words and conduct of the tenant are primary indicators in meeting these requirements.[11]

E.G.:

Application of the abandonment test can be very confusing. For example, in one case[12] a butcher closed his business for approximately ten days. The landlord did not receive one month's worth of rent, entered the leased premises, "smelled a distinct odor," and changed the locks. The landlord assumed an abandonment had occurred. The court, however, ruled that an abandonment had not occurred and that the landlord had breached the lease relieving the tenant from any further obligation thereunder. In another case,[13] a tenant told his landlord that he was leaving for two or three days to go to Montana, but did not return for eight weeks although he called the landlord during his absence and assured the landlord that he intended to return and pay the back rent owed. Despite the apparent intent not to abandon the premises, the court held an abandonment did occur and the landlord was entitled to undertake remedial actions.

One commentator suggests that despite the fact that the self-help remedy is recognized by the courts, the much more prudent action would be to follow through with a court supervised eviction proceeding to eliminate even the possibility of a wrongful eviction claim.[14]

3. Landlord's Lien

Colorado statutes create a lien in favor of a landlord upon certain personal property of the tenant for the value of unpaid rent, plus other costs.[15] The law is quite detailed and specifically excepts certain personal property from the lien. Section 38-20-102 C.R.S. provides: "The lien shall be upon the household furniture, goods, appliances and other personal property...being upon the rental premises...but exclusive of small kitchen appliances, cooking utensils, beds, bedding, necessary wearing apparel, personal or business records and documents and the personal effects of the tenant and members of his household."

Very specific requirements exist as to the assertion of the lien.[16] Enforcement of this lien requires the institution of a court foreclosure action and sale procedures. It sets strict time limits and provides for the loss of lien and/or damages if the time limits are not complied with. This procedure is complicated, costly, and riskier than an eviction action. It is also arguably unconstitutional.[17] THE LANDLORD IS URGED TO AVOID A LANDLORD LIEN ACTION WITHOUT CONSULTING WITH AN ATTORNEY.

However, there is one section of the landlord lien statute which merits brief discussion. In a situation where a tenant abandons personal property at the leased premises, the landlord may dispose of same if the following guidelines are followed:

a. Property is presumed abandoned if tenant has failed to contact the landlord for over thirty days and landlord has no knowledge that tenant intends to claim the property;
b. Fifteen days prior to selling or disposing of the abandoned property, the landlord must notify the tenant of proposed disposition;
c. The notice must contain the manner and date of disposition, and be sent to the tenant's last known address by registered or certified mail, return receipt requested, to be signed by addressee only; and
d. If the notice is returned to the landlord, a notice must be published.

A landlord is obliged to follow these requirements when disposing of abandoned property. It should be noted that unlike the other provisions of the landlord lien statute, no court proceedings are required.

II. Pre-litigation Notice: Default/Demand for Compliance or Possession

A. DEFAULT/TERMINATION DISTINGUISHED

There are three basic situations which give rise to an eviction action. The first situation is known as a DEFAULT and occurs when: (a) the tenant fails to pay rent required under the terms of tenancy; or (b) acts in a manner violating a covenant or condition under the terms of the tenancy (e.g., keeps a llama in a studio apartment when the lease states "NO PETS ALLOWED"). The second common scenario giving rise to an eviction occurs when: (a) the tenant has done nothing wrong; and (b) the terms of tenancy provide for a termination at certain time intervals or upon a certain notice; and (c) the landlord desires to terminate the tenancy. This is known as TERMINATION OF TENANCY. A third special situation involving pre-litigation notice arises in circumstances where repeated violation of a covenant occurs or substantial (usually criminal) violations of the lease transpire. They will be called SPECIAL DEFAULT NOTICES. The distinction between these three situations is important, not only because lawyers and judges love to distinguish, classify and label different situations, but also because there are different procedures for dealing with each type of problem. The default situation will be addressed first.

B. DEFAULT

1. Failure to Pay Rent

A majority of all evictions are commenced because of defaults under the terms of tenancy. The most common default is the failure to pay rent.[18] The law requires that before the tenant is technically guilty of an unlawful detention and subject to eviction, the tenant must be served with a document known as a "Written Demand," also known as a "Demand for Possession," a "Three Day Notice" or "Demand for Compliance or Possession."[19] The Demand for Compliance or Possession must give the tenant three days to either: (a) pay the rent due and owing, or (b) vacate the premises.

E.G.:

It is important to note that the failure of a tenant to pay rent on the first of the month (or other date as set forth in the agreement) does not automatically mean that a default has occurred. Prior to determining a default, the landlord must examine the lease and see if it contains some grace period within which a tenant may pay before a default occurs. A typical provision might read as follows:

> "Tenant shall pay rent to landlord on or before the first of each month during the term of this tenancy. If tenant defaults in the payment of rent, landlord may give tenant notice of such default and if tenant does not cure such default within seven days, landlord may terminate this lease on not less than three days notice."

This provision is excerpted from my own office lease. In the above scenario, a landlord would be obliged to give two notices: a "7 Day Notice" as set forth by the lease and then, after the seven days expire, a 3 Day Notice. If the landlord does not comply with this provision, it is not a proper default for an eviction action. Note, however, that unlike the 3 Day Notice, additional notices in the lease may be waived (given up) by a tenant or his agent.

Another problem to look out for when determining a default is known as WAIVER or ESTOPPEL. This situation occurs if the landlord has repeatedly accepted late or partial rent payments over a period of time. If this occurs, the landlord is said to have waived his right to receive timely or full rental payments. The court may also determine that the tenant had detrimentally relied upon the fact that the landlord was willing to accept late or partial payments and rule that the landlord is "estopped" (legally precluded by virtue of past behavior) from declaring a default. If waiver or estoppel appears to be a problem, it is not the end of the world: (a) many leases contain non-waiver clauses, although these may not be controlling, they certainly help and should be brought to the attention of the court if a tenant raises waiver or estoppel as a defense; (b) prompt payment requirements may be REVIVED after periods of accepting late payments. This can be accomplished by sending a notice of revival in letter form. This will put the tenant on notice that the landlord will no longer accept late payments. Then prospectively (not retroactively), tenant will be required to make timely payments. If the tenant fails to do so, the landlord may then proceed to declare a default.

2. Violation of Covenant or Condition

The second type of default occurs when a tenant violates a condition, rule or covenant of the tenancy other than non-payment of rent. Conditions and rules are limitless. Some common examples are: "No dogs allowed," "No waste/desecration of premises," "No loud parties," etc.

E.G.:

I remember two such covenants vividly because, working as a teenager in my grandfather's real estate office, one of my tasks was to imprint leases with a large rubber stamp stating: NO DOGS, CATS OR REPTILES. NO WATER BEDS. While I was stamping those leases, I would theorize: If one of my grandfather's tenants signed such a lease and proceeded to cohabitate (or cohibernate) with his well-behaved and lovable Gila monster, he would be in violation of a covenant or condition and would be in default under the lease. If, however, the tenant's soulmate was a Great White Salamander, he might well argue that no condition has been violated by virtue of the fact that a salamander is an amphibian and the lease is silent as to such animals. The situation could keep two of my brethren in the legal profession (who, matter-of-factly, have been referred to in similar zoological terms) busy with arguments and counter-arguments for many billable hours. However, the important point which must be made is that a violation of a covenant or condition must generally refer to a violation of a specific provision contained in a written lease.

Many pre-printed leases contain catchall covenants (e.g., [Tenant shall not] "commit, permit or suffer any objectionable or disorderly conduct, noise or nuisance whatsoever about the premises...or commit, permit or suffer anything to be done...that will disturb or interfere with the rights, comforts or conveniences of other tenants"). "Objectionable Conduct" is, of course, many things to many people. When such a catchall provision is cited as the breached covenant, a court will usually apply a reasonable man standard to determine whether a breach has occurred. Therefore, it is always better to employ a specific provision over the general.

There is no requirement that the covenant or condition be in a written lease. The covenant could very well be contained in a verbal agreement. However, the conditions of a verbal agreement will be very difficult to prove in court. Further, it can be counted on that the tenant will remember the agreement a little or quite differently from the landlord's recollection.

The law's requirements regarding this type of default are almost identical to those regarding non-payment of rent.[20] The tenant must be served with a Demand for Compliance or Possession and be given three days to alternatively comply with the condition or vacate the premises. If the tenant complies and subsequently violates the same condition or covenant, a non-curable Notice to Quit may then be provided three days prior to litigation.[21] The legislature has recently enacted special laws which are applicable to all tenancies in Colorado, making certain criminal actions by a tenant grounds for eviction without the necessity for a Demand for Compliance or Possession.[22]

3. Demand for Compliance or Possession

The Demand for Compliance or Possession (Demand), also known as the 3 Day Notice, is required to be served prior to beginning a default eviction proceeding. THE CASE WILL BE THROWN OUT OF COURT IF THIS REQUIREMENT IS NOT COMPLIED WITH. Therefore, it is essential that the statutory requirements be satisfied, TO THE LETTER OF THE LAW. The Demand is a simple one page document which notifies the tenant that within three days from receipt of the notice, the tenant must either: (a) cure the respective default, or (b) vacate the premises. A 1982 Colorado Supreme Court case had previously ruled that a tenant may waive his right to a Demand in the lease.[23] However, this holding has since been overturned by a 1983 amendment to the Colorado Statutes forbidding the waiver of a Demand.[24] Therefore, A DEMAND MUST BE SERVED EVEN IF CONTRARY LANGUAGE EXISTS IN THE LEASE.[25] The form and contents of the Demand are mandated by statute and have been elaborated upon by various cases.

4. Checklist for Demand for Compliance or Possession (Form No. 235PA)

- Written Notice[26]
- Addressed to tenant or lessee[27]
- Demand in *alternative* for: payment of rent[28] (or compliance with condition[29]) *or* possession of premises
- Description of premises[30] (preferably legal description and common address plus apartment number or unit number)
- Specific grounds for demand[31] (i.e., non-payment of rent, breach of condition)
- Time when same shall be delivered[32]

- Signed by either: all persons claiming possession (e.g., all owners, husband and wife if jointly owned property); or authorized agent or attorney.[33]

Exhibit A is a sample form, which, if completed properly, would meet all of the above requirements. This form as well as almost all other forms in this book are printed by Bradford Publishing Company, 1743 Wazee Street, Denver, Colorado 80202, (303-292-2500). They are available from the publisher and from many office supply and stationery stores for a modest price. A list of the forms and Identification Numbers are included in Appendix B.

EXHIBIT A

State of Colorado, ______1______ County of ______2______

DEMAND FOR COMPLIANCE OR POSSESSION

TO: ______3______

The Landlord set forth below hereby demands that you shall, within three days of the time this notice is served upon you, either comply with the covenant/condition stated below or deliver to the Landlord the possession of the premises known as (street address) ______4______

being Lot(s) No. ______5______ in Block No. ______5______ in ______5______

______5______ Addition/Subdivision,

in ______6______, in the ______7______* County of ______8______,

State of Colorado. The covenant/condition with which you are to comply is: (Check either or both, as applicable)

-- [a] The payment to the Landlord in the sum of $ ______(i)______ being the past due rent owed to the Landlord

9 from ______(ii)______, 19 ______, to ______(iii)______, 19 ______.

-- [b] Other covenant of the lease being violated: ______(i)______

The covenant/condition checked above constitutes a default under the terms of the Lease, which default entitles the Landlord to possession of the premises.

The rental for said premises is $ ___10___ per ___11___.

Dated this ___12___ day of ___12___, 19 ___12___.

______13______
Landlord

By: ______14______
Agent or Attorney

*If in Denver, insert "City and".

No. 235PA. Rev. 6-87. DEMAND FOR COMPLIANCE OR POSSESSION ©

Bradford Publishing, 1743 Wazee St., Denver, CO 80202 — (303) 292-2500

5. Filling out the Demand for Compliance or Possession (Form No. 235PA)

The same form of DEMAND FOR COMPLIANCE OR POSSESSION may be used for either a non-payment of rent default or a violation of condition default. Completed forms for both situations are provided in *Exhibits B* (Non-Payment of Rent) and C (Violation of Condition).

Blank 1: This should be left blank UNLESS YOU ARE IN DENVER; if so, insert "CITY and" (See *Exhibit B*).

Blank 2: Insert the county in which the property is located.

Blank 3: Insert all tenants' names which appear on the lease as well as any parties you believe are upon the premises who are not named in the lease.

Blank 4: Insert common address, e.g., "1313 Mockingbird Lane" (including unit or apartment number).

Blank 5: Insert legal description; this can be found in your deed or mortgage for the property. You can also contact your county clerk and recorder to obtain this information.

Blank 6: Insert city or village, e.g. "Golden" (unless in Denver; if in Denver, leave blank and see Blank 7).

Blank 7: Leave blank unless in Denver; if so, insert "City and".

Blank 8: Insert county in which the property is located.

Box 9: A: This box should be checked if the default is NON-PAYMENT OF RENT.

(i) Insert amount of rent past due (usually monthly rent)

(ii) Insert date when rent due (usually first of the month)

(iii) Insert end of rental period (usually last of month)

Note: If the period is more than one month, the entire period should be included. E.g. "Payment to the landlord in the sum of $400.00 being past due rent owed to landlord from April 1, 1993 to May 31, 1993." This would represent two months rent at $200.00/month.

B: This box should be checked if the default is a violation of a covenant or condition in the lease.

(i) Fill in the specific provision of lease violated and cite applicable language, e.g., "Page 2, Paragraph 5(a) prohibiting the playing of amplified barbershop quartet music after 2:00 a.m.."

Note: If tenant is in default under both A and B, both boxes may and should be checked and completed.

Blank 10: Insert periodic rent (usually monthly rent), e.g., "$600".

Blank 11: Insert period of rental payments (usually monthly), e.g., "month".

Blank 12: Insert date when notice is served; Note: The date when the Demand is actually served controls over the date that was inserted in Demand, if different.

Blank 13: Signatures of all owners; print or type names below signatures.

or

Blank 14: Signature of attorney or agent. Note: Agent or attorney must have authority to act for all owners.[34]

EXHIBIT B

State of Colorado, CITY AND County of DENVER

DEMAND FOR COMPLIANCE OR POSSESSION

TO: Thomas and Tricia Tenant and Frank Freeloader

The Landlord set forth below hereby demands that you shall, within three days of the time this notice is served upon you, either comply with the covenant/condition stated below or deliver to the Landlord the possession of the premises known as (street address) 620 West Surf Street

being Lot(s) No. 1 in Block No. 6 in ______ Addition/~~Subdivision~~,

in ______, in the City and* County of Denver,

State of Colorado. The covenant/condition with which you are to comply is: (Check either or both, as applicable)

☒ The payment to the Landlord in the sum of $ 600.00 being the past due rent owed to the Landlord from May 1, 19 95, to May 31, 19 95.

☐ Other covenant of the lease being violated: ______

The covenant/condition checked above constitutes a default under the terms of the Lease, which default entitles the Landlord to possession of the premises.

The rental for said premises is $ 600.00 per month.

Dated this 10 day of May, 1995.

Larry A. Landlord (signature)
Larry A. Landlord
Landlord

By: ______
Agent or Attorney

*If in Denver, insert "City and".

No. 235PA. Rev. 6-87. DEMAND FOR COMPLIANCE OR POSSESSION ©

Bradford Publishing, 1743 Wazee St., Denver, CO 80202 — (303) 292-2500

EXHIBIT C

State of Colorado, ______________ County of JEFFERSON

DEMAND FOR COMPLIANCE OR POSSESSION

TO: Tyrone Tenant

The Landlord set forth below hereby demands that you shall, within three days of the time this notice is served upon you, either comply with the covenant/condition stated below or deliver to the Landlord the possession of the premises known as (street address) 130 East Randolph Street, Unit a, located upon ~~being~~ Lot(s) No. 7, 8 and 9 in Block No. ______________ in George Stout's ~~Addition~~/Subdivision, in Golden, in the ______________* County of Jefferson, State of Colorado. The covenant/condition with which you are to comply is: (Check either or both, as applicable)

☐ The payment to the Landlord in the sum of $ ______________ being the past due rent owed to the Landlord from ______________, 19 ______, to ______________, 19 ______.

☒ Other covenant of the lease being violated: Page 2, Paragraph 4(a) of Lease Dated November 1, 1994 to wit: "Tenant shall be forbidden from keeping any pets or animals upon the Premise measuring longer than six feet from head to tail." Tenant currently maintains a South American Tapir upon the premises measuring 6'5".

The covenant/condition checked above constitutes a default under the terms of the Lease, which default entitles the Landlord to possession of the premises.

The rental for said premises is $ 250.00 per month.

Dated this 1st day of February, 19 95.

Loretta A. Landlord and Louis A. Landlord
Landlord

By: *Arnold A Attorney*
Arnold A. Attorney, their authorized attorney
Agent or Attorney

*If in Denver, insert "City and".

No. 235PA. Rev. 6-87. DEMAND FOR COMPLIANCE OR POSSESSION ©

Bradford Publishing, 1743 Wazee St., Denver, CO 80202 — (303) 292-2500

6. Service of Demand for Compliance or Possession

The law specifically sets forth how service of the Demand must be made.[35] It is important that these guidelines be followed; otherwise, the notice will be deemed defective and your eviction case will probably be thrown out of court.[36] Three methods of service exist: Personal, Abode and Constructive:

(a) Personal Service: Personally deliver a copy of the Notice to tenant "or other person occupying such premises."[37]

E.G.:

If more than one tenant resides on the premises, it is a good idea to deliver copies of the Notice to all of them. Although the issue of multiple tenants is often overlooked by the courts, if a tenant fails to get any notice the eviction may be deemed wrongful.

(b) Abode Service: Personally deliver a copy to a member of the tenants' family who is:
   (i) above the age of fifteen years old; and
   (ii) is residing on or in charge of the premises.[38]

(c) Constructive Service: If no one is on the premises at the time service is attempted, the notice may be "posted in some conspicuous place on the premises."[39]

E.G.:

If posting is the method used, certain things must be kept in mind: (1) be sure to securely tape, staple or otherwise affix the notice; (2) attempt to place it in a conspicuous place where the tenant will see it (if tenant rents entire house, place on the front door, if tenant rents an apartment unit, place on apartment unit's door); (3) if the notice is removed or vandalized, there may be an argument that proper notice was not given; and (4) sliding under door probably *not* adequate.

Unlike service of process (i.e., the Summons and Complaint), the law does not require that service of the notice be made by a non-party.[40] Therefore, the landlord or the landlord's representative, agent or employee may serve the notice. No clear age requirement exists as to who may serve, however it is suggested that the party be over eighteen years old.[41] REMEMBER TO MAKE PHOTOCOPIES OF THE NOTICE BEFORE YOU SERVE IT. PROPER NOTICE AND PROOF THEREOF ARE ESSENTIAL TO YOUR CASE.

EXHIBIT D

STATE OF COLORADO
____1____ County of ____2____ } ss.

I hereby certify that I served the within notice this

____3____ day of

____3____ , 19 ____

a by leaving a true copy hereof with ____

____(i)____

b by posting in a conspicuous place on the premises (i)

at ____5____

in the ____6____ County of ____7____ Colorado.

____8____

____

BRADFORD PUBLISHING CO.

7. FILLING OUT THE PROOF OF SERVICE (Back of Form No. 235PA)

On the reverse side of the Demand, there is a form for Proof of Service. This should be filled out on your copy after service. See *Exhibits D* and *E.*

Blank 1: Leave blank unless in Denver; if in Denver, insert "City and".

Blank 2: Insert name of county.

Blank 3: Date notice was served; it is advisable to also include the time of day.

Blank 4: Box A: If personal or abode service, check this box: (i) insert name of person served; physical description is also helpful.

Box B: Check if constructive service: (i) specify place of posting also helpful.

Blank 5: Address of service.

Blank 6: Insert city; if in Denver, insert "City and".

Blank 7: Insert name of county.

Blank 8: Signature of person delivering notice.

If the party delivering the notice is not going to be able to testify at trial (or default hearing), it is advisable to prepare an affidavit (a sworn statement in writing). This can be done simply by adding some language to the form, signing the document in the presence of a notary public and having the notary public notarize same. See *Exhibit E* for an example.

EXHIBIT E

STATE OF COLORADO

City and County of Denver } ss.

* I hereby certify that I served the within notice this /and affirm

10 day of

May , 19 95

[x] by leaving a true copy hereof with Trudy Tenant (16 year old daughter of Tom & Tricia). Spiked black hair, clothespin through nose, green eyes

☐ by posting in a conspicuous place on the premises

at 620 West Surf Street

in the City and County of Denver Colorado.

Larry A. Landlord

LARRY A. LANDLORD

NORA A. NOTARY

Witness my hand and official seal/

notary public

The foregoing instrument was subscribed and sworn before me this 10 day of May, 1995 by Larry Landlord.

(NOTARY SEAL)

My commission expires:

Dec. 21, 1997.

*Upon first being duly sworn,

BRADFORD PUBLISHING CO.

8. TIMING OF NOTICE

There is a certain confusion regarding which days to count and which days not to count in calculating the three day period. However, conservative construction of the applicable law yields the following rules of thumb:

(a) The day the notice was served does not count;

(b) Saturdays, Sundays and legal Holidays are excluded; and

(c) The last day of the period (i.e., third day) is included.[42]

A demand served on a Friday must give the tenant until the following Wednesday to pay the rent or surrender possession. A demand served on a Monday must give the tenant until Thursday. It is always better to err on the side of giving more than three days, rather than less. If within the three day period the tenant cures the default, then your case is over before it begins. If, however, the three day period passes without a cure, you may then proceed to the litigation stage of the process (See Chapter V).

III. Pre-litigation Notice: Special Defaults

Common events of default usually require the landlord to permit a three day cure period. However, two special types of defaults exist in which no cure period is allowed. After such defaults, a pre-litigation notice, called NOTICE TO QUIT, is required which simply alerts the tenant that a special violation has occurred and orders the tenant to leave the premises. Period. If the tenant does not comply, then the landlord may proceed to an eviction action.

The first type of special default concerns a repeat violation of a lease covenant after the tenant had previously been notified to cease such violations. The second special default involves actions by a tenant, or others on his property, which endangers persons or property and/or constitute serious criminal violations.

A. REPEAT VIOLATION OF COVENANT

1. Notice to Quit (Repeat Violation) (Form 219R)

An amendment to the FED law effective July 1, 1995, modifies the rights of tenants and the duties of landlords relative to repeated violations of lease covenants. The law provides: (a) if the landlord had previously issued a Demand for

Compliance or Possession to a tenant relative to a certain violation of a covenant; (b) the Tenant had cured the violation; and (c) the tenant subsequently commits a second violation of the same covenant, then landlord need not provide a Demand for Compliance or Possession, but, rather, may provide a Three Day Notice to Quit which does not give the tenant the opportunity to cure, and thereafter, the landlord may pursue an eviction action.[43]

This Notice to Quit is served in the same manner as the Demand for Compliance or Possession. (See Chapter II)

E.G.:

An example of the application of this new law would be as follows:

Toni Tenant, a philosophy student with an affection for punk rock, has a one (1) year written lease with Lonnie Landlord for a studio apartment near the famed Myopia Institute in Boulder, Colorado. The lease provides: "No amplified music shall be played between the hours of 7:00 p.m. and 7:00 a.m." After a particularly angst-ridden marathon class on Nietzsche which lets out at 11:00 p.m., Toni retires to her abode. She takes solace in the music of the "Remaindermen," a particularly raucous punk band comprised of disillusioned officers of the court. The next morning, she receives a Demand for Compliance or Possession from Lonnie Landlord specifying a violation of the "No amplified music" covenant in the Lease. Several months pass without incident. Late one night, Toni, after contemplating Sartre's philosophy of choice, decides she will express her existence by choosing to crank "No Exit," an existentialist "grunge" band at 2:00 a.m. The next morning, she receives a Notice to Quit from Lonnie. This Notice specifies the prior violation of the "No amplified music" covenant and the most recent violation. She ceases to play music. Lonnie subsequently files an eviction action. Toni argues that she has ceased playing music and, in fact, has now adopted a philosophy that abstains from all entertainment, including music. The court nonetheless rules against Toni and evicts her in a manner she likens to The Trial by her favorite author, Franz Kafka.

The court in the above example correctly applied the new Notice to Quit provision for repeated violations. Because this statute is new, no case law or articles relative to its application exist. A form, premised upon the language of the statute and previously adopted forms, follows the Checklist.

2. CHECKLIST FOR NOTICE TO QUIT (REPEAT VIOLATION) (Form No. 219R)

- Written notice
- Addressed to tenant or lessee
- Description of premises
- Specification of covenant/condition violated
- Date of first violation
- Date Demand for Compliance or Possession sent
- Date of subsequent violation
- Statement that Lease shall terminate
- Date when termination is effective
- Signed by landlord or agent or attorney[44]

CAUTION:

Remember that a prior Demand for Compliance or Possession must have been sent for the same violation before a landlord may use this Notice to Quit.

Exhibit F is a sample form of this Notice to Quit which would probably satisfy all statutory requirements.

EXHIBIT F

State of Colorado, ______1______ County of ______2______

NOTICE TO QUIT (Repeat Violation of Covenant)

TO: ______3______

Pursuant to Title 13-40-104(e.5), Colorado Revised Statutes, you are hereby notified by the undersigned owner that on ______4______, 19____ you were served with a Demand for Compliance or Possession by reason of a violation of covenant or condition under the terms of the Lease, specifically:
______5______

You have subsequently violated the same covenant or condition on ______6______, 19____.
THEREFORE, your tenancy of the lands and premises known as ______7______
______, in ______8______*,
County of ______9______, State of Colorado, and being also known as Lot(s) No. ______10______,
Block No. ______11______, ______12______ (Addition/Subdivision),
is hereby terminated as of ______13______, 19____, and you are accordingly notified to quit said premises and surrender possession on or before said date.
Dated ______14______, 19____.

______15______
Owner

By ______16______
Agent

*Insert name of city. If in Denver, insert "City and".

No. 219R. NOTICE TO QUIT (Repeat Violation of Covenant) ©
Bradford Publishing, 1743 Wazee St., Denver, CO 80202 — (303) 292-2500

EXHIBIT F (continued)

STATE OF COLORADO

__________ County of __________ } ss.

I hereby certify that I served the within notice this

____________________ day of

____________________, 19 ______

☐ by leaving a true copy hereof with __________

____

☐ by posting in a conspicuous place on the premises

at ____________________________

in the ____________________ County of

____________________, Colorado.

____

____

Section 13-40-104, C.R.S. Unlawful detention defined. (1) Any person is guilty of an unlawful detention of real property in the following cases:

(e) When such tenant or lessee holds over, without such permission, contrary to any other condition or covenant of the agreement under which such tenant or lessee holds, and three days' notice in writing has been duly served upon such tenant or lessee requiring in the alternative the compliance with such condition or covenant or the delivery of the possession of the premises so held.

(e.5)(I) When a tenant or lessee has previously been served with the notice described in paragraph (e) of this subsection (1) requiring compliance with a condition or covenant of the agreement, and subsequent to that notice holds over, without permission of the tenant or lessee's landlord, contrary to the same condition or convenant.

(II) A tenancy may be terminated at any time pursuant to this paragraph (e.5) on the basis of a subsequent violation. The termination shall be effective three days after service of written notice to quit.

Note: For a complete definition of unlawful detention, see the entire text of 13-40-104, C.R.S.

3. Filling Out the Notice to Quit (Repeat Violation)

A completed form of this Notice is provided in *Exhibit G.*

Blank 1: This should be left blank unless you are located in Denver; if so, insert "City and".

Blank 2: Insert the county where the real property is located.

Blank 3: Insert all tenants named in the lease as well as any parties which you believe are upon the premises who are not named in the lease.

Blank 4: Date first Demand for Compliance or Possession was served.

Blank 5: Breach of condition or covenant set forth in first Demand for Compliance or Possession and subsequently violated.

Blank 6: Insert date of subsequent violation.

Blank 7: Insert common address.

Blank 8: Insert city or town; if Denver, insert "City and".

Blank 9: Insert county.

Blank 10: Insert legal description.

Blank 11: Insert legal description.

Blank 12: Insert legal description.

Blank 13: Date when tenancy shall terminate (three days after delivery).

Blank 14: Date of service.

Blank 15: Signature(s) of all owner(s), or

Blank 16: Authorized attorney or agent signature.

Note: The back of form 219R is served and filled out the same as form 235PA. Read Chapter II for these instructions.

EXHIBIT G

State of Colorado, ____________ County of BOULDER

NOTICE TO QUIT (Repeat Violation of Covenant)

TO: TONI TENANT

Pursuant to Title 13-40-104(e.5), Colorado Revised Statutes, you are hereby notified by the undersigned owner that on October 31, 19 95 you were served with a Demand for Compliance or Possession by reason of a violation of covenant or condition under the terms of the Lease, specifically:
Paragraph 5(a) of the Lease providing "No amplified music shall be played between the hours of 7 p.m. and 7 a.m."

You have subsequently violated the same covenant or condition on January 12, 19 96.
THEREFORE, your tenancy of the lands and premises known as 1330 Dearborn Street Apartment 5A, in Boulder*, County of Boulder, State of Colorado, and being also known as Lot(s) No. 7, Block No. 5, City of Boulder, 2nd Addition (Addition/Subdivision), is hereby terminated as of January 17, 19 96, and you are accordingly notified to quit said premises and surrender possession on or before said date.
Dated January 13, 19 96.

Lonnie Landlord
LONNIE LANDLORD
Owner

By ____________
Agent

*Insert name of city. If in Denver, insert "City and".

No. 219R. NOTICE TO QUIT (Repeat Violation of Covenant) ©
Bradford Publishing, 1743 Wazee St., Denver, CO 80202 — (303) 292-2500

B. SUBSTANTIAL VIOLATION OF LEASE

1. Notice to Quit (Substantial Violation) (Form 219S)

A second recent addition to the FED law has been special provisions which are applicable to tenants who have committed violent or criminal acts on or near the leased premises. In the event of such an occurrence, no Demand for Compliance or Possession is required. Rather, only a Three Day Notice to Quit, similar to that for repeat violations of covenant, is required.[45]

The law states that it is an implied term of every lease of real property that a tenant shall not commit a "substantial violation" while in possession of the premises. A substantial violation can be any act by the tenant or "any guest or invitee" of the tenant which either:

a. occurs on or near the premises, and (i) endangers the person, or (ii) willfully and substantially endangers the property of; the landlord, co-tenant, or any person living on or near the premises, or
b. occurs on or near the premises and is a violent or drug-related felony under certain provisions of the Criminal Code.[46]

If a substantial violation occurs, a landlord may then terminate the tenancy by serving a Notice to Quit. This termination is effective three (3) days after service. This Notice does not provide a right to cure. If the tenant is served with such notice and the time period has elapsed, the landlord may proceed to an eviction action. If an eviction action is filed, the landlord has the burden of proof to show that a "substantial violation" has occurred.[47]

Two defenses are provided to such a claim of substantial violation:

a. The tenant is a victim of domestic violence, this fact has been documented in a police report, and the domestic violence is the basis for the termination notice;[48] or
b. The tenant: did not known of, <u>and</u> could not reasonably have known of, or prevented the commission of, a substantial violation by a guest or invitee but

immediately notified a law enforcement officer of his knowledge of the substantial violation.[49]

NOTE:

This is a brand new law which was hastily drafted to address "crack house" type situations in the Denver metropolitan area. Many cases are sure to follow interpreting this law. I suspect that this law will be attacked in the near future on a constitutional basis, and probably modified. Given the other remedies available to a landlord, (i.e., other defaults and violations of the lease) and the substantial burden on the landlord to basically prove the commission of a crime, I would strongly suggest that the other provisions of the FED laws be involved, if possible, rather than the Criminal Violation Provisions. If applying this method of eviction, it is strongly suggested that you contact an attorney.

This Notice to Quit is served in the same manner as the Demand for Compliance or Possession. (See Chapter II)

2. Checklist for Notice to Quit (Substantial Violation) (Form 219S)

- Written notice
- Addressed to tenant or Lessee
- Description of premises
- Grounds for termination (nature of substantial violation)
- Statement that lease will terminate
- Date when termination effective
- Signed by landlord, agent or attorney

Exhibit H is a form which incorporates the statutorily required information. Because this is a brand new law, this form is subject to change.

EXHIBIT H

State of Colorado, _____1_____ County of _____2_____

NOTICE TO QUIT (Substantial Violation)

TO: _____3_____

Pursuant to Title 13-40-107.5, Colorado Revised Statutes, you are hereby notified by the undersigned owner that on _____4_____, 19_____ you, your guest(s) and/or invitee(s) committed an act, or series of acts, which, as defined by law, constitutes a substantial violation, specifically:

☐ _____5_____

which occurred on or near the premises and endangered the person or willfully and substantially endangered the property of the landlord, any co-tenant, or any person living on or near the premises; or

☐ _____5_____

which occurred on or near the premises and constituted a violent or drug-related felony prohibited under article 3, 4, 6, 7, 9, 10, 12, or 18 of title 18, C.R.S.

THEREFORE, your tenancy of the lands and premises known as _____6_____, in _____7_____* County of _____8_____, State of Colorado, and being also known as Lot(s) No. _____9_____, Block No. _____10_____, _____11_____ (Subdivision/Addition), is hereby terminated as of _____12_____, 19_____, and you are accordingly notified to quit said premises and surrender possession on or before said date. Dated _____13_____, 19_____.

_____14_____
Owner

By _____15_____
Agent

*Insert name of city. If in Denver, insert "City and".

No. 219S. NOTICE TO QUIT (Substantial Violation) ©

Bradford Publishing, 1743 Wazee St., Denver, CO 80202 — (303) 292-2500

EXHIBIT H (continued)

STATE OF COLORADO

__________ County of __________ } ss.

I hereby certify that I served the within notice this

____________________ day of

____________________, 19 ______

☐ by leaving a true copy hereof with __________

____

☐ by posting in a conspicuous place on the premises

at ____________________________

in the ____________________ County of

____________________, Colorado.

____

____

3. Filling Out the Notice to Quit (Substantial Violation) (Form 219S)

Exhibit I is a completed Notice to Quit (Substantial Violation)

Blank 1: This should be left blank, unless you are in Denver; if so, insert "City and".

Blank 2: Insert county where real property is located.

Blank 3: Insert all tenants named in the lease, as well as any parties which you believe are upon the premises who are not named in the lease.

Blank 4: Date substantial violation occurred.

Blank 5: Specify type of substantial violation (e.g., "shot and killed Colleen Co-Tenant")

Blank 6: Insert common address.

Blank 7: Insert city or town; if in Denver insert "City and".

Blank 8: Insert county.

Blank 9: Insert legal description.

Blank 10: Insert legal description.

Blank 11: Insert legal description.

Blank 12: Date when tenancy shall terminate (three days after delivery).

Blank 13: Date of service.

Blank 14: All owner's/owners' signature, or

Blank 15: Authorized attorney or agent signature.

Note: The back of form 219S is served and filled out the same as form 235PA. Read Chapter II for those instructions.

EXHIBIT I

State of Colorado, ______________ County of PARK

NOTICE TO QUIT (Substantial Violation)

TO: TED TENANT

Pursuant to Title 13-40-107.5, Colorado Revised Statutes, you are hereby notified by the undersigned owner that on February 10, 19 95 you, your guest(s) and/or invitee(s) committed an act, or series of acts, which, as defined by law, constitutes a substantial violation, specifically:

☐ ______________

which occurred on or near the premises and endangered the person or willfully and substantially endangered the property of the landlord, any co-tenant, or any person living on or near the premises; or

XX threatened Cleopatra Co-tenant with a pistol, placing Cleopatra in fear of serious bodily injury, constituting menacing in violation of Section 18-3-206, C.R.S.

which occurred on or near the premises and constituted a violent or drug-related felony prohibited under article 3, 4, 6, 7, 9, 10, 12, or 18 of title 18, C.R.S.

THEREFORE, your tenancy of the lands and premises known as 38 Special Street, in the Town of Hartzel * County of Park, State of Colorado, and being also known as Lot(s) No. 1, Block No. 2, Town of Hartzel (~~Subdivision/Addition~~), is hereby terminated as of February 14, 19 95, and you are accordingly notified to quit said premises and surrender possession on or before said date. Dated February 11, 19 95.

Lois Landlord

LOIS LANDLORD Owner

By ______________ Agent

*Insert name of city. If in Denver, insert "City and".

No. 219S. NOTICE TO QUIT (Substantial Violation) ©

Bradford Publishing, 1743 Wazee St., Denver, CO 80202 — (303) 292-2500

IV. Pre-litigation Notice: Termination of Tenancy/Notice to Vacate

A termination of tenancy is distinguished from a default by the fact that the tenant has done nothing "wrong." Rather, the landlord is, at a legally appropriate time, simply ending the tenant's occupancy of the premises.

E.G.:

Three basic types of termination are most common:

- End of Term Lease: The tenant has a one year written lease with the landlord; term expires June 30, 1995 but the tenant fails to move out, the landlord desires the tenant out immediately.
- Holdover Tenancy: Same as example above, except: On July 1, August 1 and September 1, 1995, the tenant pays and landlord accepts rental payments; landlord then desires to get tenant out.
- Periodic Tenancy: Landlord and tenant have oral (or in rare cases, written) lease based upon an agreed periodic tenancy (e.g. week to week; month to month; year to year); landlord desires tenant out at the end of a specific period.

A. TERMINATION PROCEDURES

Depending upon the type of situation, different procedures and different time periods are applicable.

1. End of Term

This is the simplest type of termination. It is well settled law that no pre-litigation notice (Notice to Vacate) is required to be given to a tenant at the end of a term certain.[50] The tenant is deemed a trespasser and an eviction proceeding may be commenced immediately (see Chapter V).

The landlord must be careful not to ignore the fact that tenant's term has expired. If the landlord handles the situation like a tenancy still exists, for example, by collecting further rents, a court may deem a holdover tenancy to have been created. However, the simple fact that a landlord does not immediately undertake an eviction action does not, without more, create a holdover situation.

2. Holdover Tenancy

If a tenant remains on the leased premises after the expiration of a term certain and the landlord continues to treat the tenant as such (i.e., continues to collect rent or undertake other affirmative conduct), a holdover tenancy has been created.[51]The period of the holdover tenancy depends upon a number of factors which are listed in order of importance:

a. Lease: If the lease specifies the period created by a holdover situation, the lease controls.[52]

b. Term of Original Lease: If the lease is silent as to the consequences of a holdover, then the term of the original lease is important:
   - if original lease is for one year or more, the period is year-to-year tenancy;
   - if the original lease is for less than one year, the period would be equal to the lease term.

c. Rental Payment: If no other information is available the period is determined by when periodic rental payments are made (i.e., monthly, weekly, yearly).

In a holdover situation, once it is determined what period is applicable, one must then proceed under the law governing periodic tenancy. It should be noted that there is some confusion on this point. Some cases seem to suggest that a holdover creates successive "terms certain," in which case no pre-litigation Notice to Quit would be necessary. Others suggest that it is a periodic tenancy and a Notice to Quit is a prerequisite to an eviction action.[53] The better and more prudent view would be to treat all holdovers as periodic tenancies and provide the requisite Notice.

3. PERIODIC TENANCY

Service of a Notice to Vacate[54] upon the tenant is required to effect a termination of a periodic tenancy. It is of utmost importance that this Notice to Vacate be properly timed. Timing of the notice depends upon the period involved. The most typical tenancy periods and their respective notice requirements are listed below:

Year-to-Year: Three months
Month-to-Month: Ten days
Week-to-Week: Three days[55]

The law further requires that the notice must be served "not less than the respective period fixed *before the end of the applicable tenancy.*"[56] In other words, the notice must be served so that its deadline for termination coincides with an end of the applicable period. The above requirement can best be explained through example.

E.G.:

Tenant has a month-to-month tenancy which began September 1, 1994. Landlord desires to terminate tenancy, and let the premises to new tenant X effective May 1, 1995. Landlord must give tenant a Notice to Vacate ten days before the end of the monthly rental period. Thus, the notice must be given on or before April 19, 1995 to terminate the tenancy effective April 30, 1995 (remember, the day it is served does not count). If the landlord is a couple of days late, and serves the tenant on April 21, 1995, the tenancy would not be terminated on April 30, 1995, NOR WOULD IT TERMINATE ON THE NEXT

DAY, May 1, 1995. The termination must coincide with the end of a period of the tenancy.

While a mistake by the landlord in the timing of notice in a month-to-month situation may only delay termination by one more period (i.e., one month), a miscalculation involving a year-to-year tenancy may be disastrous.

NOTE:

If the Notice to Vacate is being served in connection with a building being converted into a condominium, different time periods apply. See 38-33-112 C.R.S. for more information.

B. NOTICE TO VACATE

1. CONTENTS OF NOTICE TO VACATE

The contents of a Notice to Vacate are specified by statute.[57] Unlike the Demand for Compliance or Possession, it does not give the tenant alternatives, but simply informs the tenant that the tenancy is terminated and that the premises must be vacated upon a date certain.

2. CHECKLIST FOR NOTICE TO VACATE (Form No. 219)

- Written notice
- Addressed to tenant or lessee
- Description of premises (preferably, legal description and common address)
- Particular time when tenancy shall terminate
- Signed by either:
  - all persons claiming possession (all owners), or
  - authorized agent or attorney.

Exhibit J is a sample form which, if completed properly, would meet all of the statutory requirements.

EXHIBIT J

NOTICE TO VACATE

STATE OF COLORADO
1 *County of 2 } ss.

To 3

Pursuant to Title 13-40-107, Colorado Revised Statutes, you are hereby notified by the undersigned owner that your tenancy of the lands and premises known as 4 (Street Address), in 5 (City) in the 6 * County of 7, State of Colorado, and being also known as Lot(s) No. 8, Block No. 8 8 (Addition/Subdivision), is hereby terminated as of the 9 day of 9, 19 9, and you are accordingly notified to quit said premises and surrender possession thereof on or before said date. Dated this 10 day of 10, 19 10.

11
Owner

By 12
Agent

*If in Denver, insert "City and."

No. 219. Rev. 11-86. NOTICE TO VACATE ©
Bradford Publishing, 1743 Wazee St., Denver, CO 80202 — (303) 292-2500

EXHIBIT J (continued)

STATE OF COLORADO }
_____________ County of _____________ } ss.

I hereby certify that I served the within notice this

_____________________________ day of

_____________________________ , 19 ____

☐ by leaving a true copy hereof with __________

____

☐ by posting in a conspicuous place on the premises

at _____________________________

in the _____________ County of __________
Colorado.

____

____

BRADFORD PUBLISHING CO.

13-40-107. Notice to quit. (1) A tenancy may be terminated by notice in writing, served not less than the respective period fixed before the end of the applicable tenancy, as follows:

(a) A tenancy for one year or longer, three months;

(b) A tenancy of six months or longer but less than a year, one month;

(c) A tenancy of one month or longer but less than six months, ten days;

(d) A tenancy of one week or longer but less than one month, or a tenancy at will, three days;

(e) A tenancy for less than one week, one day.

(2) Such notice shall describe the property and the particular time when the tenancy will terminate and shall be signed by the landlord or tenant, the party giving such notice or his agent or attorney.

(3) Any person in possession of real property with the assent of the owner is presumed to be a tenant at will until the contrary is shown.

(4) No notice to quit shall be necessary from or to a tenant whose term is, by agreement, to end at a time certain.

(5) Except as otherwise provided in section 38-33-112, C.R.S., the provisions of subsections (1) and (4) of this section shall not apply to the termination of a residential tenancy during the ninety-day period provided for in said section.

3. FILLING OUT THE NOTICE TO VACATE (Form 219)

Exhibit K is a completed example of a Notice to Vacate form for a month-to-month tenancy which commenced on the first of the month. *Exhibit L* is a completed example of a Notice to Vacate for a year-to-year tenancy which commenced June 1, 1992.

Blank 1: Leave blank unless in Denver; if in Denver insert "City and"

Blank 2: Insert name of county

Blank 3: Insert name(s) of tenants and those known to occupy premises

Blank 4: Insert common address

Blank 5: Insert name of city, town, village. If in Denver, leave blank.

Blank 6: Leave blank unless in Denver; if in Denver insert "City and"

Blank 7: Insert name of county

Blank 8: Insert legal description

Blank 9: Insert date of termination (typically, last day of month). Remember this date must coincide with the last date of a tenancy period as well as comporting to the respective three day, ten day or three month termination notice period.

Blank 10: Date of service

Blank 11: Signature of all owners, or

Blank 12: Signature of authorized agent or attorney

EXHIBIT K

NOTICE TO VACATE

STATE OF COLORADO

City and *County of Denver } ss.

To Troy M. Tenant

Pursuant to Title 13-40-107, Colorado Revised Statutes, you are hereby notified by the undersigned owner that your tenancy of the lands and premises known as 721 Carolina Avenue (Street Address), in ______ (City) in the City and * County of Denver, State of Colorado, and being also known as Lot(s) No. 3, Block No. 12 of Misty's Addition, Second Filing (Addition/Subdivision), is hereby terminated as of the 30th day of April, 19 95, and you are accordingly notified to quit said premises and surrender possession thereof on or before said date. Dated this 19th day of April, 19 95.

Larry A. Landlord
LARRY A. LANDLORD Owner

By ______ Agent

*If in Denver, insert "City and."

No. 219. Rev. 11-86. NOTICE TO VACATE ©

Bradford Publishing, 1743 Wazee St., Denver, CO 80202 — (303) 292-2500

EXHIBIT L

NOTICE TO VACATE

STATE OF COLORADO
_____*County of Arapahoe } ss.

To Tonto Tenant

Pursuant to Title 13-40-107, Colorado Revised Statutes, you are hereby notified by the undersigned owner that your tenancy of the lands and premises known as 1492 Columbus Avenue (Street Address), in Littleton (City) in the _____* County of Arapahoe, State of Colorado, and being also known as Lot(s) No. 1, Block No. 4 Silver Heights Subdivision (Addition/Subdivision), is hereby terminated as of the 31st day of May, 19 95, and you are accordingly notified to quit said premises and surrender possession thereof on or before said date. Dated this 28th day of February, 19 95.

Lone R. Landlord
LONE R. LANDLORD Owner

By _____ Agent

*If in Denver, insert "City and."

No. 219. Rev. 11-86. NOTICE TO VACATE ©

Bradford Publishing, 1743 Wazee St., Denver, CO 80202 — (303) 292-2500

4. Service of Notice to Vacate

The requirements of service of a Notice to Vacate are identical to that of the Demand for Compliance or Possession (see Chapter II). The same rules regarding timing of the Demand for Compliance or Possession apply to the Notice to Vacate WITH ONE MAJOR EXCEPTION: IN PERIODS INVOLVING OVER SEVEN DAYS (E.G., 10 DAY NOTICE) WEEKENDS AND HOLIDAYS DO COUNT TOWARDS THE PERIOD.[58] However, if the last day of said period is a weekend day or legal holiday, the period is run until the end of the next day which is not a Saturday, Sunday, or legal holiday.

5. Filling Out the Proof of Service

This, too, is identical to that of the Demand for Compliance or Possession (see Chapter II).

V. Complaint

A. CONTENTS OF COMPLAINT

If, after the landlord has complied with the applicable pre-litigation notice requirements, the appropriate time period has passed and the tenant has failed to comply with the request set forth in the demand or notice, a complaint may then be prepared, filed and served upon the tenant. The filing of a complaint officially commences an eviction proceeding. The law sets forth specific requirements regarding the contents of a complaint filed in an eviction case, as well as additional matters that may be included.[59]

1. Checklist for Complaint (Form No. 94)

- Caption: contains court, action number and parties[60]
- Statement as to jurisdiction (county court – Claim is under $10,000)
- Description of property with reasonable certainty (legal, common address, plus apartment or unit number)
- Name of person(s) in possession or occupancy
- Include basis of tenancy (e.g., written lease)
- The grounds for recovery

- Request for recovery of premises (e.g., request to kick tenants out)[61]
- Amount of rent/damages due
- Request for recovery of damages due (including present and future damages, costs and any other relief which plaintiff is entitled to)
- Statement referring to a Demand for Possession or Notice to Quit, if applicable[62]
- Notarized signature, address and phone number of plaintiff

  or
- Signature of attorney, with requisite information

Exhibit M is a sample form which, if completed properly, would meet all of the above requirements.

EXHIBIT M

1 COURT, 2 COUNTY 3, COLORADO
Civil Action No. 4 Div./CtRm 5

COMPLAINT (UNLAWFUL DETAINER)

6 v. 7

Plaintiff Defendant

Plaintiff, for its complaint, states and alleges as follows:

1. Plaintiff is the owner or agent for the owner of the premises in the 8 ** County of 9, State of Colorado, described as follows: 10.

2. Defendant leased and occupied the premises 11 (pursuant to a written lease, a copy of which is attached hereby as Exhibit A and incorporated herein by reference) 12 (pursuant to a verbal month-to-month tenancy) 13 (pursuant to a verbal tenancy at will)* at a monthly rental of $ 14, payable (in advance)* on the 14 day of each month.

Check either or both as applicable:

15☐ 3. Defendant failed to pay the monthly rental due on the following date(s) (i)

and as of this filing is indebted to the Plaintiff for past due rent in the sum of $ (ii).

16☐ 4. Defendant has violated the terms and conditions of the lease by failing to comply with the following covenants or conditions of said lease: (i).

17 5. Plaintiff properly served a written demand for compliance with the terms of the lease or possession, (a copy of which is attached hereto as Exhibit B and incorporated herein by reference) pursuant to Section 13-40-104, C.R.S., on the 18 day of 18, 19 18, but Defendant has failed or refused to comply with said demand or to give up possession.

6. The Defendant unlawfully, and wrongfully holds possession of the described premises without the consent of the Plaintiff. Rent will continue to accrue at the rate of $ 19 per day until Plaintiff regains possession of the described premises.

7. The amount demanded by Plaintiff (or the monthly rental value) does/does not* exceed $10,000.00. 20

8. The Defendant is not engaged in the military service of the United States and is engaged in a civilian occupation.

WHEREFORE, Plaintiff requests judgment for recovery of possession of the premises, for the rent, if any, due or to become due, for present and future damages and costs, and any other relief to which Plaintiff is entitled.

21
Plaintiff's/Attorney's Signature (Type Plaintiff's name address and tele. no. below)

23
Attorney's name, address, tele. no., Reg. no.

Subscribed and sworn to by 22 before me this ______ day of ______, 19 ______, in the ______ County of ______, State of ______.
My commission expires ______.

22
Officer administering oath

*Strike inapplicable language
**If in Denver, insert "City and".

2. Filling out the Complaint (Form No. 94)

Exhibit N is a sample complaint filled out in a non-payment of rent situation. *Exhibit O* is a sample complaint under a violation of covenant situation where the tenant is paid up on the rent. *Exhibit P* is a sample complaint pursuant to a termination of a period tenancy.

Blank 1: Insert court. This would either be "County" (damages under $10,000) or "District" (damages over $10,000).

Blank 2: Leave blank unless in Denver; if in Denver insert "City and".

Blank 3: Insert name of county.

Blank 4: Leave this blank. When the case is filed, the clerk will either stamp an Action Number on the complaint or tell you what number to fill in. This number is important and must be on all other papers filed in your case.

Blank 5: Leave this blank. The clerk will stamp or tell you the division and courtroom, if applicable

Blank 6: Insert the landlord's name (Note: if more than one owner, insert all names). If landlord is other than a natural person (i.e., corporation) see section 5 at the end of this chapter.

Blank 7: Insert all tenants' names, as well as all others known to be occupying the property.

Blank 8: Leave blank unless in Denver; if in Denver, insert "City and".

Blank 9: Insert name of county.

Blank 10: Insert common address, legal description (include apartment or unit number if applicable).

Line 11: If a written lease exists, leave this line and attach a photocopy of the lease to all copies of the complaint. On the bottom of the first page of the lease, write or type "EXHIBIT A". If a written lease does not exist, cross out this line.

Lines 12 & 13: If a written lease exists, cross out these lines. If a verbal periodic tenancy exists, cross out the line which is not applicable. (Chapter IV A for a discussion of Periodic Tenancy.)

Blank 14: Insert the monthly rental rate and the day it was payable (usually, the first of the month). Typically, rents are paid in advance; thus the "in advance" language should remain unless rent was paid in arrears (this is rare).

Box 15: This should be checked if there was a default for non-payment of rent.

(i) Insert date when rent is due e.g., "May 1, 1995"; if more than one time, insert additional dates.

(ii) Insert the amount of rent due *as of* the filing date. Calculation of this amount requires a per diem (per day) calculation of the rent. Use the following formula: monthly rent ÷ days in month = rent per diem × number of days from default to filing. For example: $250 monthly rent ÷ 30 days = $8.33 per day × 12 days = $100.00.

E.G.:

Calculation of this amount is subject to some controversy. Almost all leases provide that the rent is payable monthly, in advance. Thus, after the first of the month *the entire* month's rent is due for that month or any portion thereof. It can be argued that the amount past due is the *full* monthly rent which has not been paid. Despite the language of leases, courts have been less than open to claims for full rent if the landlord is seeking to dispossess a tenant prior to the end of that period.

If any other damages are claimed, such as destruction of the premises, a claim for same may be inserted here or a separate page may be incorporated by reference.

Box 16: This box should be checked if tenant defaulted by violating a covenant or condition of tenancy.

(i) Insert specific provision of lease which was violated and quote specific language from lease (see *Exhibit N*). If any other damages are claimed they may be inserted here or a separate page may be incorporated by reference.

Note: If the tenant is in breach of both the rent provisions and other covenants, check and complete both boxes 15 and 16.

Line 17: If (as in most cases) a pre-litigation demand was required (Form 235PA), attach a photocopy and label it "EXHIBIT B". However, if this is a termination of tenancy pursuant to a Notice to Vacate (Form 219), it should be attached as *Exhibit B* and the alteration as set forth in *Exhibit P* should be included. If pre-litigation notice was a Notice to Quit (Substantial Violation) make the appropriate alteration and attach a copy of the Notice as *Exhibit B.* If a Notice to Quit (Repeat Violation) was used, attach both the first Demand for Compliance and the Notice to Quit as *"Group Exhibit B."*

Blank 18: Insert day which Notice was served upon tenant.

Blank 19: Insert per diem calculation (see example under Box 15).

Line 20: In most situations, the amount will be under $10,000 and be in County Court. If so, strike out "does". If it is over $10,000, the claim must be brought in the District Court and you must strike "does not".

Line 21: Signature of plaintiff or attorney.

Line 22: VERIFICATION to be filled out by notary Public.[63]

Line 23: Attorney signature (if applicable).

3. Exhibits to Complaint

Although not legally required, it is highly advisable to include a copy of the written lease (if one exists), as well as a copy of all pre-litigation notices served upon the tenant as exhibits to the complaint.

4. Jury Demand

Landlords are almost always better off with a bench (judge) trial than a jury trial. A jury trial is available for eviction actions,[64] if desired. If a jury is requested, type "Jury Demand" or "Plaintiff demands a trial by jury" on top of the complaint or as additional paragraph after paragraph 8. An additional fee will be charged.

5. Landlord is "Non-natural" Person

All examples in this text assume that the landlord is a natural person, or persons. If however, the landlord is a different type of entity (e.g., corporation, limited liability company, limited or general partnership), depending on the specific fact, representation by an attorney may be required (see § 12-5-112, C.R.S.). There is an exception for close (small) corporations (see § 13-1-129, C.R.S.), and a general partnership may arguably represent themselves (see § 7-60-109, 110, C.R.S.). However, if the landlord is not a natural person, consultation with an attorney is strongly suggested.

EXHIBIT N

COUNTY COURT, CITY AND COUNTY OF DENVER, COLORADO
Civil Action No. 95 C 1234 Div./CtRm

COMPLAINT (UNLAWFUL DETAINER)

LOUISA L. LANDLORD
and
LENNY L. LANDLORD
Plaintiff

v.

THEODORE A. TENANT
Defendant

Plaintiff, for its complaint, states and alleges as follows:

1. Plaintiff is the owner or agent for the owner of the premises in the City and ** County of Denver, State of Colorado, described as follows: Apt. 7, 444 St. James Place; Legally described as: Lot 6, Block 2, Johnson's Addition, 3rd filing, County of Denver.

2. Defendant leased and occupied the premises (pursuant to a written lease, a copy of which is attached hereby as Exhibit A and incorporated herein by reference) ~~(pursuant to a verbal month-to-month tenancy) (pursuant to a verbal tenancy-at will)~~* at a monthly rental of $ 800.00, payable (in advance)* on the 1st day of each month.

Check either or both as applicable:

☒ 3. Defendant failed to pay the monthly rental due on the following date(s) June 1, 1995, July 1, 1995 and as of this filing is indebted to the Plaintiff for past due rent in the sum of $ 1,200.00.

☐ 4. Defendant has violated the terms and conditions of the lease by failing to comply with the following covenants or conditions of said lease: ______.

5. Plaintiff properly served a written demand for compliance with the terms of the lease or possession, (a copy of which is attached hereto as Exhibit B and incorporated herein by reference) pursuant to Section 13-40-104, C.R.S., on the 2nd day of July, 19 95, but Defendant has failed or refused to comply with said demand or to give up possession.

6. The Defendant unlawfully, and wrongfully holds possession of the described premises without the consent of the Plaintiff. Rent will continue to accrue at the rate of $ 26.67 per day until Plaintiff regains possession of the described premises.

7. The amount demanded by Plaintiff (or the monthly rental value) ~~does~~/does not* exceed $10,000.00.

8. The Defendant is not engaged in the military service of the United States and is engaged in a civilian occupation.

WHEREFORE, Plaintiff requests judgment for recovery of possession of the premises, for the rent, if any, due or to become due, for present and future damages and costs, and any other relief to which Plaintiff is entitled.

Louisa L. Landlord Lenny L. Landlord
Plaintiff's/Attorney's Signature (Type Plaintiff's name address and tele. no. below)
Louisa L. Landlord and
Lenny L. Landlord
1212 Penthouse Row
Denver, CO 303-555-5555

Attorney's name, address, tele. no., Reg. no.

Subscribed and sworn to by Louisa L. and Lenny L. Landlord before me this 15th day of July, 19 95, in the City and County of Denver, State of Colorado.

My commission expires September 9, 1999.

Natalie E. Notary
Officer administering oath
Natalie E. Notary

*Strike inapplicable language
**If in Denver, insert "City and".

No. 94. Rev. 1-91. COMPLAINT (UNLAWFUL DETAINER)

Bradford Publishing, 1743 Wazee St., Denver, CO 80202 — (303) 292-2500

EXHIBIT O

COUNTY COURT, ______________ COUNTY GUNNISON, COLORADO
Civil Action No. 95 C 1235 Div./CtRm ______

COMPLAINT (UNLAWFUL DETAINER)

LAURA L. LANDLORD v. TIMOTHY TENANT

Plaintiff / Defendant

Plaintiff, for its complaint, states and alleges as follows:

1. Plaintiff is the owner or agent for the owner of the premises in the ______________** County of Gunnison, State of Colorado, described as follows: 3000 Elk Avenue, Unit A, Crested Butte, CO. Legally Described as: Lot 17, Block 2, Red Lady Subdivision, County of Gunnison, CO.

2. Defendant leased and occupied the premises ~~(pursuant to a written lease, a copy of which is attached hereby as Exhibit A and incorporated herein by reference)~~ (pursuant to a verbal month-to-month tenancy) ~~(pursuant to a verbal tenancy at will)~~* at a monthly rental of $ 1,000.00, payable (in advance)* on the 1st day of each month.

Check either or both as applicable:

☐ 3. Defendant failed to pay the monthly rental due on the following date(s) ______________ and as of this filing is indebted to the Plaintiff for past due rent in the sum of $ ______.

☒ 4. Defendant has violated the terms and conditions of the lease by failing to comply with the following covenants or conditions of said lease: Page 5, Paragraph 15 which prohibits playing any loud music between the hours of 10:00 P.M. and 8:00 A.M. Defendant's rock band, the "Moody Miners", could be heard playing from 9:00 P.M. to 4:00 A.M. by anyone within a two mile radius of the premises.

5. Plaintiff properly served a written demand for compliance with the terms of the lease or possession, (a copy of which is attached hereto as Exhibit B and incorporated herein by reference) pursuant to Section 13-40-104, C.R.S., on the 21st day of September, 19 95, but Defendant has failed or refused to comply with said demand or to give up possession.

6. The Defendant unlawfully, and wrongfully holds possession of the described premises without the consent of the Plaintiff. ~~Rent will continue to accrue at the rate of $ ______ per day until Plaintiff regains possession of the described premises.~~

7. The amount demanded by Plaintiff (or the monthly rental value) ~~does~~/does not* exceed $10,000.00.

8. The Defendant is not engaged in the military service of the United States and is engaged in a civilian occupation.

WHEREFORE, Plaintiff requests judgment for recovery of possession of the premises, ~~for the rent, if any, due or to become due,~~ for present and future damages and costs, and any other relief to which Plaintiff is entitled.

Laura L. Landlord
Plaintiff's/Attorney's Signature (Type Plaintiff's name address and tele. no. below)
Laura L. Landlord
1242 1st Street
Crested Butte, CO 555-5555

____
Attorney's name, address, tele. no., Reg. no.

Subscribed and sworn to by Laura Landlord before me this 30th day of September, 19 95, in the ______ County of Gunnison, State of Colorado.
My commission expires July 14, 1997.

Natalie N. Notary
Officer administering oath
Natalie N. Notary

*Strike inapplicable language
**If in Denver, insert "City and".

Bradford Publishing, 1743 Wazee St., Denver, CO 80202 — (303) 292-2500

EXHIBIT P

COUNTY COURT, ______ COUNTY BOULDER, COLORADO
Civil Action No. 95 C 1717 Div./CtRm ______

COMPLAINT (UNLAWFUL DETAINER)

LISLE L. LANDLORD v. THORNTON T. TENANT

Plaintiff Defendant

Plaintiff, for its complaint, states and alleges as follows:

1. Plaintiff is the owner or agent for the owner of the premises in the ______** County of Boulder, State of Colorado, described as follows: 12 Tungsten Avenue, Nederland, CO; Legally described as: that portion of the south ½ southwest ¼, section 8, township 1 south, range 72 west, 6th p.m.

2. Defendant leased and occupied the premises ~~(pursuant to a written lease, a copy of which is attached hereby as Exhibit A and incorporated herein by reference)~~ (pursuant to a verbal month-to-month tenancy) ~~(pursuant to a verbal tenancy at will)~~* at a monthly rental of $ 100.00, payable (in advance)* on the 1st day of each month.

Check either or both as applicable:

☐ 3. Defendant failed to pay the monthly rental due on the following date(s) ______

and as of this filing is indebted to the Plaintiff for past due rent in the sum of $ ______.

☒ 4. Defendant has ~~violated the terms and conditions of the lease by failing to comply with the following covenants or conditions of said lease:~~ failed to vacate the premises after being duly notified of the termination of his month-to-month tenancy effective March 31, 1995.

5. Plaintiff properly served a written ~~demand for compliance with the terms of the lease or possession~~ Notice to Quit (a copy of which is attached hereto as Exhibit B and incorporated herein by reference) pursuant to Section 13-40-~~104~~108 C.R.S., on the 20th day of March, 19 95, but Defendant has failed or refused to comply with said demand or to give up possession.

6. The Defendant unlawfully, and wrongfully holds possession of the described premises without the consent of the Plaintiff. Rent will continue to accrue at the rate of $ 3.22 per day until Plaintiff regains possession of the described premises.

7. The amount demanded by Plaintiff (or the monthly rental value) ~~does~~/does not* exceed $10,000.00.

8. The Defendant is not engaged in the military service of the United States and is engaged in a civilian occupation.

WHEREFORE, Plaintiff requests judgment for recovery of possession of the premises, for the rent, if any, due or to become due, for present and future damages and costs, and any other relief to which Plaintiff is entitled.

Lisle L. Landlord
Plaintiff's/Attorney's Signature (Type Plaintiff's name address and tele. no. below)
Lisle L. Landlord
1000 Folsom Street
Boulder, CO 5551212

Arnold A. Attorney
Attorney's name, address, tele. no., Reg. no.
Arnold A. Attorney
A. Reg. #:66666
Tungsten Towers Penthouse
Nederland, CO 5555555

Subscribed and sworn to by Lisle L. Landlord before me this ______ day of ______, 19 ______, in the ______ County of ______,
State of ______.
My commission expires ______.

______
Officer administering oath

*Strike inapplicable language
**If in Denver, insert "City and".

No. 94. Rev. 1-91. COMPLAINT (UNLAWFUL DETAINER)
Bradford Publishing, 1743 Wazee St., Denver, CO 80202 — (303) 292-2500

VI. Summons

A. CONTENTS OF SUMMONS

A Summons is a document which informs an individual that a legal action has been commenced against the defendant. Further, it informs the defendant of the time and place the defendant must file an answer and when to appear in court (RETURN DATE). The Summons must be prepared at the same time as the complaint. Technically, service of the Summons brings the defendant under jurisdiction of the court. Once served, the court may enter judgment(s) against the defendant without further notice.[65] It should be noted that a Summons for Forcible Entry and Unlawful Detainer is different than for a *conventional* county court case.

E.G.:

Effective January 1, 1994, the Colorado Supreme Court adopted a new form for Summons in Forcible Entry and Unlawful Detainer. Under C.R.C.P. Rule 310, use of this form is mandatory in County Court.[66]

If the claim exceeds $10,000.00, the action must be filed in District Court. Another Summons, Form No. 83D, is designed for use in District Court, but not shown in this book. Both

Summons are available at Bradford Publishing Company. MAKE SURE YOU HAVE THE APPROPRIATE FORM.

A plaintiff in an eviction action is responsible for causing the defendant to be served with the Summons, as well as a copy of the complaint and answer form, before any further proceedings may occur in the court case.[67]

1. Checklist for Summons (Form No. 83)

- Caption: contains court, action number and parties
- Command to defendant to appear before court
- Time and place for appearance
- Statutory statement
- Date[68]
- Issued by clerk of court or attorney[69]
- Copy of Answer form

Exhibit Q is a sample form which, if completed properly would meet all of the above requirements.

NOTE:

Remember to include a blank Answer form with Summons. This is required by C.R.C.P. Rule 304(b).

EXHIBIT Q

COUNTY COURT, ________1________ COUNTY, COLORADO
Case No. ____2____

SUMMONS IN FORCIBLE ENTRY AND UNLAWFUL DETAINER

Plaintiff(s) 3

vs.

15

Defendant(s) 4

To the above named Defendant(s): Take notice that

1. On ________5________, 19____ at ________ o'clock ____.M., in the ____6____ County Court, ____7____, Colorado, the court may be asked to enter judgment against you as set forth in the complaint.
2. A copy of the complaint against you and an answer form which you must use if you file an answer are attached.
3. If you do not agree with the complaint, then you must either:
   a. Go to the court, located at ________8________, ________, Colorado, at the above date and time and file the answer stating any legal reason you have why judgment should not be entered against you, or
   b. File the answer with the court before that date and time.
4. When you file your answer, you must pay a filing fee to the Clerk of the Court.
5. If you file an answer, you must give or mail a copy to the Plaintiff(s) or the attorney who signed the complaint.
6. If you do not file with the court, at or before the time for appearance specified in this summons, an answer to the complaint setting forth the grounds upon which you base your claim for possession and denying or admitting all of the material allegations of the complaint, judgment by default may be taken against you for the possession of the property described in the complaint, for the rent, if any, due or to become due, for present and future damages and costs, and for any other relief to which the Plaintiff(s) is (are) entitled.
7. If you want a jury trial, you must ask for one in the answer and pay a jury fee in addition to the filing fee.
8. If you want to file an answer or request a jury trial and you are indigent, you must appear at the above date and time, fill out a financial affidavit, and ask the court to waive the fee.

Dated at ____9____, Colorado, this ______ day of ____10____, 19____.

Clerk of the Court

by ____11____
Deputy Clerk

____12____
Attorney for Plaintiff(s) (if applicable) (print name, registration number, address, and telephone number)

____13____
Address(es) of Plaintiff(s)

____14____
Telephone Number(s) of Plaintiff(s)

This summons is issued pursuant to Rule 303, Rules of County Court Civil Procedure, as amended, and section 13-40-111, C.R.S. A copy of the complaint must be served with this summons. This form should be used only for actions filed under Colorado's Forcible Entry and Detainer Act.

To the clerk: if this summons is issued by the Clerk of the Court, the signature block for the clerk, deputy and the seal of the court should be provided by stamp, or typewriter, in the space to the left of the attorney's name.

WARNING: ALL FEES ARE NON-REFUNDABLE. IN SOME CASES, A REQUEST FOR A JURY TRIAL MAY BE DENIED PURSUANT TO LAW EVEN THOUGH A JURY FEE HAS BEEN PAID.

No. 83. Rev. 10-94. SUMMONS IN FORCIBLE ENTRY AND UNLAWFUL DETAINER
Bradford Publishing, 1743 Wazee St., Denver, CO 80202 — (303) 292-2500

2. Filling out the Summons (Form No. 83)

Exhibit R is a completed sample summons.

Blank 1: If in Denver insert "City and County of Denver". If not, insert name of county only.

Blank 2: Insert civil action number and courtroom number, if available (obtain this from clerk)

Blank 3: Insert all plaintiffs

Blank 4: Insert all defendants

Blank 5: Insert date and time (obtain this from clerk)

Blank 6: Insert name of county

Blank 7: Insert name of city

Blank 8: Insert address of court, and common name e.g. "Boulder County Justice Center, 1777 6th Street, Boulder, Colorado"

Blank 9: Insert name of city or town in which you are filing this.

Blank 10: Leave blank. Clerk issuing summons will fill this in; if not filled in, insert date summons was issued.

Blank 11: Leave blank (clerk will fill this in).

Blank 12: If attorney is issuing summons, attorney must sign and insert requisite information below.

Blank 13: Insert address of Plaintiff

Blank 14: Insert telephone number of Plaintiff

Blank 15: Insert information to aid in service of summons, e.g., "Sheriff please serve Defendant at: 1276 Second Street, 3rd Floor, Nederland, Colorado before 8:00 a.m. or after 5:00 p.m."

EXHIBIT R

COUNTY COURT, Gunnison COUNTY, COLORADO
Case No. 94 C 1235

SUMMONS IN FORCIBLE ENTRY AND UNLAWFUL DETAINER

Plaintiff(s) Laura L. Landlord

vs.

Defendant(s) Tommy A. Tenant

Sheriff please serve defendant at:
3000 Elk Avenue, Gunnison, CO
Before 11:00 A.M. or after 2:00 A.M.

To the above named Defendant(s): Take notice that

1. On July 10, 19 95 at 9 o'clock A .M., in the Gunnison County Court, Gunnison, Colorado, the court may be asked to enter judgment against you as set forth in the complaint.
2. A copy of the complaint against you and an answer form which you must use if you file an answer are attached.
3. If you do not agree with the complaint, then you must either:
   a. Go to the court, located at 200 East Virginia, Gunnison, Colorado, at the above date and time and file the answer stating any legal reason you have why judgment should not be entered against you, or
   b. File the answer with the court before that date and time.
4. When you file your answer, you must pay a filing fee to the Clerk of the Court.
5. If you file an answer, you must give or mail a copy to the Plaintiff(s) or the attorney who signed the complaint.
6. If you do not file with the court, at or before the time for appearance specified in this summons, an answer to the complaint setting forth the grounds upon which you base your claim for possession and denying or admitting all of the material allegations of the complaint, judgment by default may be taken against you for the possession of the property described in the complaint, for the rent, if any, due or to become due, for present and future damages and costs, and for any other relief to which the Plaintiff(s) is (are) entitled.
7. If you want a jury trial, you must ask for one in the answer and pay a jury fee in addition to the filing fee.
8. If you want to file an answer or request a jury trial and you are indigent, you must appear at the above date and time, fill out a financial affidavit, and ask the court to waive the fee.

Dated at Gunnison, Colorado, this 2nd day of July, 19 95.

Clerk of the Court

by ______________________
Deputy Clerk

____
Attorney for Plaintiff(s) (if applicable) (print name, registration number, address, and telephone number)

805 E. Happy Lane, Gunnison, CO
Address(es) of Plaintiff(s)

555-1855
Telephone Number(s) of Plaintiff(s)

This summons is issued pursuant to Rule 303, Rules of County Court Civil Procedure, as amended, and section 13-40-111, C.R.S. A copy of the complaint must be served with this summons. This form should be used only for actions filed under Colorado's Forcible Entry and Detainer Act.

To the clerk: if this summons is issued by the Clerk of the Court, the signature block for the clerk, deputy and the seal of the court should be provided by stamp, or typewriter, in the space to the left of the attorney's name.

WARNING: ALL FEES ARE NON-REFUNDABLE. IN SOME CASES, A REQUEST FOR A JURY TRIAL MAY BE DENIED PURSUANT TO LAW EVEN THOUGH A JURY FEE HAS BEEN PAID.

No. 83. Rev. 10-94. SUMMONS IN FORCIBLE ENTRY AND UNLAWFUL DETAINER
Bradford Publishing, 1743 Wazee St., Denver, CO 80202 — (303) 292-2500

B. FILING OF COMPLAINT/ISSUANCE OF SUMMONS

Once the Complaint, Summons and Exhibits are prepared, they are ready to be filed, issued and served. BE SURE TO MAKE SEVERAL PHOTOCOPIES OF ALL THESE DOCUMENTS. A good rule is to make four copies of each document plus one for each additional defendant.

Take all documents to respective clerk of court. The clerk will collect your filing fees assign your case a civil action number, file your original Complaint, file stamp all of your copies and issue your Summons. An attorney handling the case is also empowered to issue a summons.[70] The clerk will also give you the information regarding the return date, time and place; this must be inserted into the appropriate blanks upon the summons.

C. WHERE TO FILE

The eviction action MUST BE FILED IN THE COUNTY WHERE THE PROPERTY IS LOCATED. As discussed previously, if the amount sought is over $10,000, it must be filed with the district court. If under $10,000, it should be filed with the county court.[71]

D. SERVICE OF PROCESS

Each defendant named in the case must be served with their own individual copy of the Summons and Complaint. This is known as "Service of Process." This is essential because if a defendant is not served, he/she is not subject to the court's orders. Improper service will hold up a case while the problem is being resolved, so it is better to get *good service* the first time around. The rules regarding proper service upon a party are set forth in Section 13-40-112, C.R.S. and Rules 4 and 304, C.R.C.P. These are reprinted in the Appendix. A review and understanding of these rules is suggested.

E. AUTHORIZED PROCESS SERVERS

Process can either be served by:

1. The sheriff of the county where service is made; or

2. Any person over the age of 18 not a party to the action.

E.G.:

The service must be made by a disinterested person i.e., not a relative, employee, agent, etc. Typically, this is a private process server. It is suggested that the sheriff be used because: (a) it lends an air of authority to the proceeding; (b) the sheriff is relatively inexpensive and cost-effective; and (c) if there is a dispute as to service, the sheriff makes a very credible witness.

Bring copies of the Complaint, the original Summons and a blank Answer form to the sheriff. Be prepared to pay a service fee (plus mileage) to the sheriff and leave sufficient copies with the sheriff. The sheriff may also request that a separate form setting forth information relevant to service be filled out. Practices vary by county.

F. METHOD OF SERVICE

Like other civil cases, the process in an eviction case may be by personal service.

E.G.:

Personal service is preferable because it will give the court jurisdiction to enter both possession and monetary judgments.

---

1. Requirements for Personal Service

a. Delivery of process to the defendant personally; or
b. Leaving a copy of process at the defendant's dwelling, house or place of abode with some member of the defendant's family over the age of 18; or
c. Leaving a copy of process at the defendant's usual place of business with the defendant's "stenographer, bookkeeper or chief clerk"; or

d. Delivering a copy of process to an agent authorized by law to receive same.[72]

Unlike other civil cases, process may also be served by "posting."[73] This is also known as "constructive service." This must be accomplished by a person authorized to serve process and MAY ONLY BE CARRIED OUT AFTER THE SERVER HAD MADE A "DILIGENT EFFORT TO MAKE PERSONAL SERVICE."

E.G.:

Service by posting is only adequate to bestow the court with jurisdiction over the property, i.e., an order for possession may be entered, but not for monetary damages.

---

2. Requirements for Posting

a. Diligent effort made for personal service
b. Post copy of Summons and Complaint
c. Post in conspicuous place on the premises
d. Mail copy of the Summons to the defendant NO LATER THAN THE DAY AFTER THE DAY ON WHICH THE COMPLAINT WAS FILED, by first class mail.[74]

E.G.:

Clarify with your process server who wil mail the copy of the Summons and Complaint. Depending upon who you use, either you or the process server may accomplish the mailing of Process.

G. TIMING OF SERVICE

The law requires that the return date on the Summons shall not be less than five days, nor more than ten days from the date of issuance. Service of Summons, whether by posting or personal service, must be made upon the defendant at least five (5) days before the return date. Therefore, there is only a small window of one to five days in which to serve the defendant. If it is anticipated that the defendant might have to be served by posting a copy of the Summons, it should be mailed to the defendant immediately after issuing it and filing the complaint.[75] If service is by posting, the court will not consider any claim for money damages and is only empowered to consider the issue of possession of the premises.[76]

H. RETURN OF SERVICE

The Return of Service portion on the back of the Summons Form 83 must be completed by the process server and filed with the court.[77] The court will not take any action on a case without a Return of Service in the file. It is the responsibility of the Landlord to establish with the process server who will be filing the Return and to make sure it is filed before the return date. Sometimes the sheriff or private process server will prepare their own form of proof of service. Verify this when placing papers for service.

CAUTION:

If the process server does not use the Return of Service on the back of form 83 for proof of service, be sure that the statement made by the server includes a statement that the Summons, Complaint AND AN ANSWER form were served. This relatively new requirement could be overlooked.

VII. Tenant's Pre-trial Procedures

A tenant facing eviction proceedings must keep in mind that the single, most important thing a tenant can do is to pay attention to the situation. DO NOT IGNORE phone calls, pre-trial notices or process.

A. EARLY LETTERS/PHONE CALLS

At least 75% of the time before a landlord even considers pursuing legal action, the landlord will attempt to contact the tenant by phone or letter regarding an actual or perceived problem. A large portion of problems are resolved with early communication.

Tenants should respond promptly to phone calls or letters from the landlord. There is nothing that will force the onset of litigation more rapidly than a stonewalling tenant. If a problem exists regarding such things as the timely payment of rent or a barking dog, the tenant should be aware of the interests and concerns of the landlord.

E.G.:

Although a five-day delay in the payment of rent may seem minimal to a tenant, to a landlord relying upon this sum to pay the monthly mortgage, non-payment can literally put the landlord in default of the mortgage and place the building in jeopardy of foreclosure.

The tenant should explain to the landlord any problems or special circumstances which brought about the problem and suggest resolution of the matter. Written correspondence is recommended. Letters confirming the contents of any telephone conversations should be sent. In your communications, do not offer to undertake any payments or other obligations which you know you are not going to be able to honor. If a resolution or compromise is reached, the agreement should be memorialized in writing. This agreement need not be fancy or formal, but should contain the following:

1. Checklist for Agreement
   - Date
   - Parties to agreement (landlord and tenant)
   - Statement of obligations
   - Property description
   - Recitation as to what original agreement/lease required i.e., the bargain of each party: "Tenant will give X, Landlord will give Y"
   - Recitation of agreement (e.g., reduced payments, different timing, etc.)
   - Date when agreement begins/ends
   - What happens if parties fail to comply with agreement
   - Signatures of parties

An example of an agreement is included as *Exhibit S.*

E.G.:

There is a certain controversy as to whether a rent modification agreement is really a legally enforceable contract if the landlord does not get something other than what he already has (e.g., the rent). This is legally known as lack of consideration. It is advisable to make sure that each side gets something new, for instance the tenant gets more time, the landlord gets interest payments on late rental amounts (other than what he is entitled to under the lease).

EXHIBIT S

THIS AGREEMENT is entered into this 10th day of March, 1995 by and between LOUIS LANDLORD (Landlord) and TROY TENANT (Tenant) in consideration of the respective undertakings herein contained and other good and valuable consideration.

1. Landlord and Tenant entered into an Apartment Lease for Apartment No. 5, 451 Melrose Avenue, Boulder, Colorado on June 1, 1994 (Lease) wherein Tenant is required to pay the Landlord a monthly rental payment of Five Hundred and no/100 Dollars ($500.00) due on the first of every month.

2. On February 15, 1995, Tenant lost his job as a Pizza Delivery Clown at Pizza Circus.

3. Tenant failed to pay his March rental payment which constitutes a breach of the Lease. However, Landlord is willing to waive such breach pursuant to the conditions and obligations contained in this Agreement.

4. Tenant now has a full-time job as a street performance mime on the Pearl Street Mall.

5. Landlord agrees to accept and Tenant agrees to pay the March rent plus interest of Ten and no/100 Dollars ($10.00) on or before April 1, 1995, along with the regular April 1, 1995 rental payment.

6. All remaining terms and conditions of the Lease are in full force and effect. Subsequent defaults shall not be deemed waived by this Agreement.

Louis Landlord
LOUIS LANDLORD

Troy Tenant
TROY TENANT

B. RECEIPT OF PRE-LITIGATION NOTICE

As discussed in Chapters II, III and IV, prior to almost all eviction proceedings, the tenant is entitled to a pre-litigation notice. Typically this is either a Demand for Compliance or Possession, a Notice to Vacate or Notice to Quit. A tenant's possible action depends upon what type of notice is sent.

1. Demand for Compliance or Possession

The first thing a tenant should do upon receipt of a Demand for Compliance or Possession is check the lease to see if any longer or additional notices are required.

E.G.:

If a period longer than three days is required by the Lease, the tenant should inform the landlord of that provision. Document this communication.

If nothing else is required by the lease, the next step is to double-check the time period with regard to the notice. This is particularly important if you were served by posting.[78] If served by posting, it is possible that the notice was posted some time ago and the cure period has already expired.

E.G.:

As long as the landlord has complied with the statutory requirements of posting, there is no requirement that the tenant actually see the Notice within the 3 day period. In other words, a tenant can be on a two week vacation and be legally served with a 3 Day Notice which expires before the tenant returns.

Next, evaluate the demand contained in the notice. Is the demand correct? Is there a default? If so, you must decide whether to comply with the demand (pay past due rent, or comply with covenants or conditions) or vacate the premises. NOTE: IF YOU VACATE THE PREMISES, YOU MAY STILL BE LIABLE FOR SUBSEQUENT RENTAL PAYMENTS THROUGH THE TERM OF YOUR LEASE![79] If you decide to cure the default, contact the landlord and inform him of your intentions immediately. Make arrangements to cure the default before the three day period has expired. The payment or cure must be timely and for the full amount, no partial payments.[80] A letter should accompany payment. *Exhibit T* is an example of such a letter.

CAUTION:

Because the period allowed by the statute is only three days from receipt of the notice, time is of the essence. A tenant responding to a notice should make sure the letter is received by the landlord within the appropriate time. Suggested methods include personal delivery or overnight messenger service.

EXHIBIT T

TOMMY TENANT
1222 Avian Drive
Durango, Colorado

December 5, 1994

Mr. Leroy Landlord
1545 Jeep Street
Durango, Colorado

VIA OVERNIGHT DELIVERY

Dear Mr. Landlord:

I am in receipt of your Demand for Compliance or Possession dated and received by me on December 4, 1994. Please be advised that the alleged violation of the condition set forth on page 21, paragraph 15 of the lease prohibiting "Pets or birds of over 6 feet tall on the premises" has been cured as of this date. For your information, Otto, my former pet ostrich, was sold to Billy Bob's Boot Factory today. If there are any further problems regarding this issue, please contact me.

Merry Christmas,

Tommy Tenant

Tommy Tenant
Phone: (303 555-BOOT)

2. Notice to Vacate/Notice to Quit

Unlike a Demand for Compliance or Possession, a Notice to Vacate or Notice to Quit gives no alternatives and simply states the tenancy is terminated and requires that the premises be vacated by a specific date. Upon receipt of a Notice to Vacate, the time periods involved and required should be examined (see Chapter IV). If there is a defect in the timing or method of service a defense may exist. A Notice to Quit which contains factual flaws or is improperly employed (e.g. no prior Demand sent in conjunction with "Repeat Violation Notice to Quit;" no substantial violation in conjunction with "Substantial Violation Notice to Quit") may also be defective and serve as a basis for a defense. Otherwise, the landlord is entitled to terminate the tenancy and dispossess the tenant of the property.

C. RECEIPT OF PROCESS

If no cure or vacation of the premises has occurred after the requisite pre-litigation notice period has passed, the sheriff or private process server will serve the tenant with process (see Chapter VI). The Summons will specify the return date which serves both as:

- the deadline for the tenant to file the Answer, and
- the date and time which the tenant must appear to set trial upon the case.[81]

If the tenant agrees with everything in the Complaint and does not dispute any of its facts, has no defenses and no counterclaims (claims against the landlord), there is not much more the tenant can do except to show up at the return date, watch the judge enter a judgment and be ready to get dispossessed by the sheriff within approximately two to fourteen days. However, it is rare that a tenant agrees with everything that a landlord alleges, or does not have a defense. It is essential that a timely Answer be prepared and filed.

D. ANSWER

The Answer is a document which is filed with the court and served upon the plaintiff by the defendant. The Answer must be filed "at or before the time specified for (Defendant's) appearance," i.e., the return date.[82] The statute mandates the contents of the Answer and gives a suggested form.[83] Because a large majority of eviction cases are brought in county court, all answer forms presented in this book are for county court. A written Answer must be filed by every defendant wishing to contest an eviction action. If an Answer is not filed, it is conclusively presumed that the defendant admits all of the allegations contained in the Complaint.[84] Any Answer which fails to specifically admit or deny the allegations of the Complaint will be deemed to have admitted the allegations.[85] Finally, the Answer must contain each and every defense which the defendant intends to rely upon.[86]

1. Defenses to Eviction

The following is not an exhaustive list of defenses to evictions, but only some of the most common and most recognized by the courts:[87]

a. No Default

Obviously, if no default exists under the lease, an eviction will not be successful. Typically, a defense under this category would involve alleging facts showing that:

- the rent at issue was timely and fully paid or tendered,[88] or
- the covenants claimed to have been violated were cured in a timely manner or had, in fact, never occurred.[89]

b. Waiver

A waiver is a situation wherein a default did in fact occur but the landlord, either by word or conduct, explicitly or implicitly, assented to it or "let it go."[90] A waiver may be demonstrated by a written agreement,[91] verbal statements,[92] or by conduct.[93] If a waiver is established, this will serve as a defense to an eviction action served upon the alleged default.

E.G.:

The following is an example of a waiver defense:

The lease requires that rent be paid on the first of the month; the tenant has consistently paid the rent to the landlord on the tenth of the month; the landlord never complained. The landlord then brings a lawsuit against the tenant on the fifth of the month, claiming breach of the lease. The tenant may assert a defense of waiver.

---

c. Defective Notice/Defective Service of Process

Notice is not required before serving a Summons and Complaint if the term of the lease has ended. However, any other type of termination requires proper pre-litigation notice.[94] Notice may be defective for several other reasons as discussed previously.

- improper time period,[95]
- improper party(s) named or served,[96]
- improper method of service,[97]
- improper contents,[98] or
- improper type of notice.

A tenant seeking to assert a defense of defective notice should review the statutory requirements for notice and allege all defects which the facts give rise to (see Chapters II, III and IV). A successful allegation of defective notice will cause the eviction action to be thrown out and will require the landlord to comply with the notice requirements and refile the action.

E.G.:

It should be noted that not all defects in notices will amount to a valid defense. For example, cases have held that a demand in the notice for more rent than is actually due will not invalidate the notice, provided that some rent is in fact due and owing. In another case, a tenant argued that a notice which was set forth on two separate pages did not comply with the statutory notice requirements. This argument was rejected by the court.[99]

Defective service of process will also constitute a defense. It must be underscored that an objection based upon improper service of process is a jurisdictional issue. A court must be informed of the improper service issue prior to any other defenses or arguments upon the merits of the case. If a defendant appears in court and responds to merits, the defendant waives the defense of improper service. Because of the potential damages of losing an important defense, consultation with an attorney is suggested if a service problem is suspected.

d. Constructive Eviction

A constructive eviction situation arises when a tenant is denied the full use and enjoyment of the leased premises, or when the premises are rendered unfit for occupancy as a result of an action or omission by the landlord, and such action or omission causes the tenant to abandon the leased premises. The defense of constructive eviction would come into play in a situation where a landlord sues a tenant for rent or other damages after a tenant has moved out of the premises because of its condition.[100] Two major requirements must be satisfied before a court will find constructive eviction:

- Denial of use of premises/premises rendered unfit for occupancy;[101] and
- Abandonment of premises by tenant within reasonable time[102]

The landlord should always be notified in writing at the earliest possible time of a perceived constructive eviction problem. A constructive eviction defense imposed as an afterthought, subsequent to receiving a notice or process, will almost surely fail.

E.G.:

This pitfall can best be illustrated by example.

<u>Example 1:</u> The tenant takes possession of the premises on May 1. The tenant pays May rent and June rent. On June 15, the tenant sends a letter to the landlord informing the landlord that the premises are uninhabitable because of a malfunctioning heating system which keeps the premises at a constant temperature of 115° fahrenheit and that the tenant intends to abandon the premises. The tenant vacates the property and fails to pay July rent. The landlord

then institutes an action. A constructive eviction defense will probably succeed.

Example 2: The same as Example 1 above, only the tenant sends the letter to landlord *after* the landlord has instituted an eviction action. Constructive eviction will probably fail.

---

e. Breach of Covenant of Quiet Enjoyment

This defense is very similar to constructive eviction, however an actual abandonment is not necessary.[103] A breach of this covenant may be found in leases which do not contain an agreement to the contrary.[104] The requirement for breach would be: "A disturbance of a lessee's possession by the lessor which renders the premises unfit for occupancy for the purposes for which they were leased".

E.G.:

Cases finding a breach of the implied covenant of quiet enjoyment include: flooding from pipes in an architectural studio, rodent infestation and structural problems, heating and plumbing problems in combination with a collapsed ceiling.

The constructive eviction and quiet enjoyment defenses are some of the most rapidly evolving areas of landlord/tenant law. They are also some of the most complex. Even judges and experienced lawyers tend to confuse the two issues. Therefore, if a constructive eviction or quiet enjoyment defense is anticipated, IT IS IMPORTANT TO CONSULT AN EXPERIENCED REAL ESTATE ATTORNEY.

Finally, there exists some confusion in case law as to whether these concepts may be employed as defenses or only as counterclaims to evictions. This relates to whether the lease covenants were deemed to be independent or dependent.[105] Once again, this issue is quite complex and beyond the scope of this book.

E.G.:

A contract with "Dependent Covenants" means that the breach of one promise by a landlord (e.g., to provide promised space or services) allows a tenant to suspend performance on tenant's promise (e.g., to pay rent).

A contract with "Independent Covenants" means that despite the breach of promise by one party, the other party may not suspend performance but must perform and seek a separate remedy.

f. Implied Warranty of Habitability

The warranty of habitability doctrine implies a warranty in all leases that the premises will meet certain minimum standards of safety and health. Many jurisdictions recognize an implied warranty of habitability in residential leases.[106] These safety and health standards vary depending upon the jurisdiction. If this warranty is breached, the tenant has a defense to non-payment of rent. However, IT IS WELL-SETTLED LAW THAT COLORADO DOES NOT RECOGNIZE IMPLIED WARRANTY OF HABITABILITY.[107] Therefore, do not raise this as a defense.

g. Failure to Mitigate

A tenant may be responsible for subsequent rent after default and dispossession of the premises if the lease so provides.[108] However, a landlord is under a duty to take reasonable steps to mitigate the possible damages.[109]

E.G.:

Mitigation means cutting your losses. A landlord cannot simply sit idle and watch the damages add up. A landlord must take reasonable actions to minimize damages such as attempting to relet the premises for the balance of the term of the lease.

While the defense of failure to mitigate may not serve to help the tenant retain possession, it may serve to reduce damages claimed due and owing by the landlord. Recent cases have found a failure to mitigate where landlord refused to accept a sublessee or assignee for an invalid or arbitrary reason, or accepted an entry premium from a subsequent tenant and failed to apply the amount to the former tenant's account. However, it must be kept in mind that mitigation duties, like all other duties of landlord and tenant, may be modified (though not eliminated) by the language in the lease.

E.G.:

A typical clause modifying a landlord's duty to mitigate would read as follows:

"If the tenant shall fail to pay rent and the landlord re-enters the premises, the landlord may then re-let the premises at the current commercial rental rate, and upon such other terms and conditions as the landlord, in its sole discretion, may deem advisable."

---

2. Counterclaims

A counterclaim is any claim which a defendant (in this case, the tenant) has against the plaintiff (landlord). A counterclaim must be filed at the time the Answer is filed.[110] Counterclaims will not preclude a landlord from obtaining possession of the premises. However, a successful counterclaim may serve to reduce or eliminate money judgments for rent and in some circumstances, may even exceed the claims of the landlord.

a. Breach of Quiet Enjoyment/Constructive Eviction

The same theories discussed under the defenses section may be brought as counterclaims. The measure of damages in a breach of quiet enjoyment claim is the difference between original rent and the fair rental value of the premises after the breach.[111] The measure of damages on a constructive eviction claim is the rental value of the unexpired term of the lease, less the rent reserved, plus other losses resulting from wrongful eviction. As with the related defenses, because the issues are quite complicated it is suggested that the counsel of an attorney experienced in these matters be consulted.

b. Unjust Enrichment/Conversion/ Outrageous Conduct

Typically, a written lease will state that all improvements a tenant makes upon the premises accrue to the benefit of the landlord and the tenant is not entitled to reimbursement for them. However, if the lease is silent as to this aspect, there is at least one case which holds that a tenant's improvements to the property can be the subject of claim by the tenant against the landlord.[112] Such a situation might occur if a tenant installed ceiling fans in an apartment and was then evicted. The tenant might then claim the value of the fans in a counterclaim. Another possible counterclaim might be for conversion. This claim would arise for damage or loss to the tenant's personal property which occurred by virtue of landlord's affirmative actions or omission with regard to the premises. Other counterclaims may include intentional infliction of emotional distress or outrageous conduct.[113]

E.G.:

Conversion counterclaim could be of several varieties:

a. A tenant's personal property is removed from the leased premises by the landlord, without authority of law. The landlord throws the property on the curbside. The property is stolen or damaged.

b. A tenant's personal property is legally within the leased premises. The landlord, intentionally, or with reckless disregard, damages the personal property belonging to the tenant.

c. An intentional infliction of emotional distress counterclaim could arise in situations where the landlord repeatedly makes harassing telephone calls and visits demanding the rent at all hours of the day and evening. The landlord threatens to have thugs kick the tenant out in the middle of the night. These actions result in verifiable mental or physical ailments.

This list is not exhaustive. Counterclaims and defenses are very fact-oriented. If some sort of wrong or damage is done to a tenant by a landlord there is probably a cause of action and remedy. The best resource for this type of claim would be relevant case law or consultation with an attorney experienced in these matters.

3. CHECKLIST FOR ANSWER (Form No. 63)

- Must be in writing[114]
- Caption: contains court, action number and parties
- Set forth grounds on which claim for possession is based
- Admission or denial of all the material allegations of the complaint
- Presentation of <u>every</u> defense
- Counterclaim (if applicable); Cross-claim (if applicable)
- Jury demand (if applicable)
- Signature[115]
- Telephone number[116]

NOTE:

Effective January 1, 1994, Rule 304, C.R.C.P. provides that, except in certain cases of service by publication, a blank Answer form must be provided to the Tenant at the time the Summons and Complaint are served. Rule 308 requires that the form and content are no longer suggested but are instead mandatory.

Exhibit U is a sample form which, if filled in correctly, would comply with the statutory requirements.

EXHIBIT U

COUNTY COURT, 1 COUNTY, COLORADO
Case No. 2

ANSWER UNDER SIMPLIFIED CIVIL PROCEDURE (including counterclaim(s) and cross claim(s)

Plaintiff(s) 3
vs.

Defendant(s) 4

The Defendant(s) 5,
answer(s) the complaint as follows:

1. The amount of damages claimed to be due to the Plaintiff(s) by the complaint in this action is not due and owing for the following reasons:

6

OR the personal property claimed by the Plaintiff(s) should not be ordered to be turned over for the following reasons:

7

OR the injunctive relief requested by the Plaintiff(s) should not be allowed for the following reasons:

2. (If applicable) the Defendant(s), 8 a),
assert(s) the following counterclaim(s) or setoff(s) against the Plaintiff(s), 8 b):

9

3. (If applicable) the Defendant(s) 10 a),
assert(s) the following cross claim(s) against 10 b),
named Defendant(s) (you are limited to the jurisdiction of the court):

11

12 4. If a counterclaim is asserted above, you must check one of the following statements:
- ☐ The amount of the counterclaim does not exceed the jurisdiction of the court (County Court filing fee required).
- ☐ The amount of the counterclaim exceeds the jurisdiction of the court, but I wish to limit my recovery to the jurisdiction of the court (County Court filing fee required).
- ☐ The amount of the counterclaim exceeds the jurisdiction of the court, and I wish the case transferred to the District Court (District Court filing fee required).

13 5. The Defendant(s) does (do) ☐ does (do) not ☐ demand trial by jury (if demand is made a jury fee must be paid).

WARNING: ALL FEES ARE NON-REFUNDABLE. IN SOME CASES, A REQUEST FOR A JURY TRIAL MAY BE DENIED PURSUANT TO LAW EVEN THOUGH A JURY FEE HAS BEEN PAID.

Note: All Defendants filing this answer must sign unless the answer is signed by an attorney.

14
Signature(s) of Defendant(s)

15
Address(es) of Defendant(s)

16
Telephone number(s) of Defendant(s)

17
Signature of Attorney for Defendant(s) (if applicable) (print registration number, address, and telephone number)

No. 63. Rev. 12-93. ANSWER UNDER SIMPLIFIED CIVIL PROCEDURE (including counterclaim(s) and cross claim(s)
Bradford Publishing, 1743 Wazee St., Denver, CO 80202 — (303) 292-2500

4. Filling Out the Answer (Form No. 63)

Unfortunately, the required form makes it quite difficult to include the statutorily required information. It is essential to insert all of the requisite information because of the rule of law that any allegations of material facts not denied in the Answer are deemed admitted.[117] If more space is needed, additional information can be typed on 8½ x 11 paper and referenced on the Answer form as an attachment. *Exhibit V* is a filled-in sample form having a defense of tender of payment and a counterclaim for breach of warranty of quiet enjoyment.

Blank 1: Insert name of county.

Blank 2: Insert case number (see Complaint caption).

Blank 3: Insert all plaintiffs (see Complaint).

Blank 4: Insert all defendants (see Complaint).

Blank 5: Insert names of defendant(s) filing Answer.

Blank 6: • Important: Insert admissions or denials to each material allegation contained in the Complaint. The best way to do this is to read each paragraph of the Complaint and either admit or deny it. (Note: You may admit parts of paragraphs and deny others.) E.g., "Defendant admits Paragraphs 1, 7 and 8 of the Complaint and denies the remaining allegation of Complaint except Defendant admits that a verbal month-to-month tenancy was entered into."

• Insert additional facts which support your argument that the amount claimed is not due to the plaintiff (See Defenses, Section 1).

• State that you are attaching any documents which support your argument.

Blank 7: • Strike "personal property" and insert "premises".

• Insert additional facts which support the argument that the premises should not be turned over (e.g., no default under lease, defective Notice to Vacate; defective Demand for Compliance or Possession, waiver by plaintiff, etc.).

Note: In most cases you should strike the next line "OR the inunctive relief requested by the Plaintiff, etc." See Rule 365, C.R.C.P. for an explanation as to when injunctive relief is available in county court.

Blank 8: Insert:

a) Defendant's name; and

b) Plaintiff's name

Blank 9: Insert any facts supporting counterclaims or set-offs. (See Section 2.)

Blank 10: Insert:

a) Defendant's name; and

b) Plaintiff's name

Blank 11: Insert cross-claims against Co-Defendants, if any.

Blank 12: If you assert counterclaim, check:

a) If claim is worth less than $10,000.00.

b) If claim is over $10,000.00, but wish to keep case in county court and limit any recovery to $10,000.00 or less.

c) If claim is over $10,000.00, and you wish to have case transferred to district court

Blank 13: Check the first box if a jury is desired; check the second box if a jury is not desired. (See *Jury Demand* at the end of this chapter for more information.)

Blank 14: Insert your signature

Blank 15: Insert your address

Blank 16: Insert your phone number

Blank 16: Attorney information, if applicable

Note: If you mail the Answer form, fill out the Certificate of Mailing and keep a copy for your records. This verifies that you mailed it to the plaintiff or attorney for the plaintiff.

EXHIBIT V

COUNTY COURT, DENVER COUNTY, COLORADO
Case No. 94 C 1234

ANSWER UNDER SIMPLIFIED CIVIL PROCEDURE (including counterclaim(s) and cross claim(s)

Plaintiff(s) LOUISA L. LANDLORD AND LENNY L. LANDLORD
vs.

Defendant(s) THEODORA A. TENANT

The Defendant(s) Theodora A. Tenant,
answer(s) the complaint as follows:

1. The amount of damages claimed to be due to the Plaintiff(s) by the complaint in this action is not due and owing for the following reasons:

Tenant admits Paragraphs 1, 7 & 8 of Complaint and denies remaining allegations of Complaint. Tenant states monthly rental was reduced to $600 per month on May 1, 1994 as per attached Exhibit A. Rental payments for June and July, 1994 were tendered but rejected by Landlord. No additional amounts are due and owing.

OR the ~~personal property~~ Premises claimed by the Plaintiff(s) should not be ordered to be turned over for the following reasons:

a) No default existed under the lease, all rents due were tendered on a timely basis but not accepted by Landlord; b) Landlord's 3 Day Notice was defective. Notice was served upon my daughter on 7/2/94 and this action commenced on 7/3/94; c) 3 Day Notice was improperly served: daughter receiving service was three (3) years of age (in violation of C.R.S. § 13-40-106).

OR ~~the injunctive relief requested by the Plaintiff(s) should not be allowed for the following reasons:~~

2. (If applicable) the Defendant(s), THEODORA A. TENANT,
assert(s) the following counterclaim(s) ~~or setoff(s)~~ against the Plaintiff(s), LOUISA L. LANDLORD AND LENNY L. LANDLORD:

a) Landlord has breached Warranty of Quiet Enjoyment, by virtue of constant construction in basement from beginning of tenancy. Damages suffered: $3,000.00 (Three Thousand and no/100 Dollars).

~~3. (If applicable) the Defendant(s)~~ ----------,
~~assert(s) the following cross-claim(s) against~~ ----------,
~~named Defendant(s) (you are limited to the jurisdiction of the court).~~

4. If a counterclaim is asserted above, you must check one of the following statements:
   - ☒ The amount of the counterclaim does not exceed the jurisdiction of the court (County Court filing fee required).
   - ☐ The amount of the counterclaim exceeds the jurisdiction of the court, but I wish to limit my recovery to the jurisdiction of the court (County Court filing fee required).
   - ☐ The amount of the counterclaim exceeds the jurisdiction of the court, and I wish the case transferred to the District Court (District Court filing fee required).

5. The Defendant(s) does (do) ☒ does (do) not ☐ demand trial by jury (if demand is made a jury fee must be paid).

WARNING: ALL FEES ARE NON-REFUNDABLE. IN SOME CASES, A REQUEST FOR A JURY TRIAL MAY BE DENIED PURSUANT TO LAW EVEN THOUGH A JURY FEE HAS BEEN PAID.

Note: All Defendants filing this answer must sign unless the answer is signed by an attorney.

Theodora A. Tenant
Signature(s) of Defendant(s)

Apt. #7, 444 St. James Place, Denver, CO
Address(es) of Defendant(s)

555-1111
Telephone number(s) of Defendant(s)

Signature of Attorney for Defendant(s) (if applicable) (print registration number, address, and telephone number)

No. 63. Rev. 12-93. ANSWER UNDER SIMPLIFIED CIVIL PROCEDURE (including counterclaim(s) and cross claim(s)
Bradford Publishing, 1743 Wazee St., Denver, CO 80202 — (303) 292-2500

5. Filing the Answer

a. When to File/Where to File

The Answer must be filed with the clerk of the court on or before the return date listed on the summons.[118] It is suggested that it be filed at least the day before the return date so that if, on the return date the clerk's office is crowded, you will not be rushed. An Answer fee must be paid at the time the Answer is filed. As of this time, the fee in county court is $26.00. This is subject to change. If you cannot afford the fee, tell the clerk. The clerk will require that the judge approve a pauper's petition before you can file. REMEMBER TO MAKE SEVERAL PHOTOCOPIES OF THE ANSWER. Present the original Answer to the clerk and have the clerk file-stamp your copies. A copy of the Answer must be served upon the plaintiff prior to filing or within forty-eight hours after filing.[119]

NOTE:

If you are filing the Answer the day before your appearance date, you can simply hand a copy of your Answer to the plaintiff in court. Service for this section means hand delivery or first class mail. If you mail the Answer, fill out the Certificate of Mailing on the back of the form.

b. Jury Demand

The landlord and/or tenant are entitled to request a jury trial if they so desire. An additional jury fee must be paid at the time the demand is filed (presently $50 in county court). In district court, the rules allow a jury demand to be filed "not later than ten days after service of the last pleading." Because of the conflicting time periods in an eviction proceeding, such timing may not be possible. (See §§ 13-40-113, 114 C.R.S.) In county court, the jury demand must be endorsed upon the Answer or Complaint. It may also be made orally at the time of the initial appearance. In District Court, it may either appear on the pleadings or in a separate document. Once a jury is demanded, the other party must either pay the requisite jury fee or file a Notice of Waiver of the Right to Trial by Jury.[111]

VIII. Return Date Procedure

A. RETURN DATE/SETTING OF TRIAL

1. Return Date

On the return date, the parties must appear at the time and place designated on the Summons. If a sufficient Answer has been filed, the case is deemed *at issue* and the case will be set for trial. If no Answer has been filed, and all other requirements have been complied with, the court will enter a default judgment against the tenant.

2. Setting of Trial

Unlike other types of cases, eviction actions were intended by the legislature to provide a summary proceeding to determine possession. Thus, an accelerated trial date is contemplated under the statute and is proper.[121] When setting the trial date, the court will probably give the parties a date one to five days from the return date.[122] The trial date may be the date of the return if both parties and the court are ready. It is advisable to be ready for trial on the return date just in case this occurs. A party may be required to post a bond or other security if he/she requests a delay in trial for longer than five days. The amount of security must be equal to the amount that a non-moving party would be damaged. It should be pointed out that this bond requirement is at the discretion of the court and only good cause must be shown.[123]

B. DEFAULT

If the defendant fails to file a written answer on or before the return date, a default judgment in favor of the plaintiff may be obtained. The judgment may be for possession of the premises and the amount due, including interest, costs and other items provided by statute or contract.[124]

E.G.:

The procedure involved in asking for a default judgment is known as a MOTION. Motions may be either oral or written. In county court, written motions are not permitted without the permission of the court.[125] On the other hand, in district court, motions are almost always written. Because a majority of all evictions are pursued in county court, this guide will focus on county court procedures.[126]

1. Oral Motion for Default Judgment

At the court hearing on the return date, the plaintiff should approach the judge when the case is called. Report to the judge that no answer is on file, the defendant is not present in court and request that a default judgment be entered against the defendant. The judge will determine if procedures were followed properly and all requirements met before entering a default judgment. The plaintiff must be prepared to provide the following specific information and proof on the return date when asking for a default judgment.

2. Notice/Personal Jurisdiction

The judge must be provided with proof that the defendant has been adequately notified and is under the jurisdiction of the court. Two different proofs are required:

- Pre-Litigation Notice; and
- Service of Process.

Pre-litigation notice may be proven by presenting a copy of the Demand, Notice to Vacate or Notice to Quit with the proof of service (form on back of Demand or Notice) completed. If the party serving the document will be present in court, this form need not be an affidavit (sworn statement). If the party who served the notice is not in court, the proof should be prepared as shown in *Exhibit E* or a separate affidavit should be prepared.

Service of process will be proven by the Proof of Service which has been filed either by the sheriff or private process server. The plaintiff should check the file before the return date to make sure it is in the file. If it is not in the file, the respective server should be notified and a duplicate proof of service should be obtained. Remember that if service was only by posting, the court will only have jurisdiction to enter an order for possession and not for monetary damages.[127]

3. Venue

The law specifically requires that the judge ascertain that proper venue exists before a default judgment is entered.[128] Venue means the place of the trial. In all cases affecting real property, such as an eviction, venue is proper in the county where the property is located. Therefore, simply inform the judge of the location of the property and the fact that it is located in that county.

4. Damages

If monetary damages are sought in addition to possession, additional documentation may be required. The lease, setting forth the monthly rent, preferably with original signatures, should be available for the court's review. Any further documentation such as a rent register should also be available. Finally, a party with personal knowledge of the amounts claimed should attend. In the alternative, an affidavit detailing the claimed damages signed by an individual with personal knowledge is recommended. This requirement is especially important if the complaint filed was signed by an attorney and was not verified by the plaintiff.

Although courts vary as to what they will require in a default situation, a plaintiff armed with the above information and a verified complaint will be well prepared to satisfy a judge's inquiries prior to entry of a default order.

IX. Trial

A complete discussion of civil trial procedure is well beyond the scope of this book. However, this guide will attempt to list and describe some of the most important trial preparations and procedures. These are the procedures that tend to take most non-attorneys by surprise, no matter how many episodes of *L.A. Law* and *People's Court* a person has seen. As with the rest of this book, this section should not be viewed as a substitute for professional consultation and/or representation.

E.G.:

"Bench trials" are trials which occur when the judge is the finder of fact and no jury is present. This section will deal only with bench trials and not jury trials. If a jury trial is contemplated, consultation and representation by an experienced attorney is highly recommended.

A. CHRONOLOGY OF TRIAL

Although many of the parties to an eviction appear pro se (on behalf of themselves), the judge is still required by law to adhere to the rules of civil procedure and evidence which govern the conduct of a trial. Additionally, there are many practices which are governed by custom or practice and are not written in the law.[129] Some judges may relax evidentiary or procedural requirements in pro se situations; however, this depends almost entirely on the judge. If a pro se party is litigating against an attorney, it is very likely that the judge will feel more pressure to enforce the procedural and evidentiary rules.

There is no rule or statute setting forth the order of trial in Colorado. However, the courts almost universally stick to the following order:

- Opening statement of plaintiff
- Opening statement of defendant
- Presentation of plaintiff's direct evidence
- Presentation of defendant's direct evidence (in defense to plaintiff's claim and presentation of counterclaim, if any)
- Presentation of plaintiff's rebuttal evidence
- Closing argument by plaintiff
- Closing argument by defendant[130]

Note: Parties are also entitled to cross-examination during their adversaries case-in-chief. In other words, the parties are allowed to ask questions of their opponent's witnesses.

B. OPENING STATEMENT

This is an opportunity for the parties to tell the court what they intend to prove in their cases. The statements are not for the purpose of introducing evidence in the case but rather serve as a guide to what will be presented. The opening statement should preview the witnesses and exhibits which will be presented, the evidence which they will elicit, and the theory of the claim or defense.[131]

C. DIRECT EVIDENCE

Basically, all evidence which the court considers must come through either testimony of a witness or exhibits which are admitted into evidence. The parties therefore must review the elements to be proven (or rebutted) in their respective cases and plan which document or witness will satisfy the respective requirements.

1. Landlord's Direct Evidence

In a typical eviction, the elements which a landlord must prove are:

a. Ownership of property, existence and terms of tenancy (month-to-month oral; written lease);
b. Default of tenancy by tenant or termination by landlord or tenant;
c. Proper notification of tenant (Demand for Compliance or Possession);
d. Failure to cure default; and
e. Damages (the amount of rent owing).

The sources of evidence a landlord would normally employ include:

a. Written lease (original) (and authenticating evidence);[132]
b. Copy of Demand or Notice;
c. Proof of Service of Demand or Notice (original);
d. Testimony of party serving Demand or Notice; and
e. Testimony of party with personal knowledge as to defaults/absence of cure and damages.

2. Tenant's Direct Evidence

In a typical eviction action, the tenant must attempt to rebut the elements listed immediately above. Additionally, if a defense or counterclaim is possible, the tenant must learn the elements required by the respective defense or counterclaim and prove those.

D. REBUTTAL EVIDENCE

This evidence is presented in reaction and in opposition to the direct evidence. It must not present evidence as to issues not raised in the direct case it is rebutting.

E.G.:

Rebuttal may occur either through adding new witnesses or recalling witnesses called in the case-in-chief. An example of a case when a rebuttal is proper follows:

Tenant, in its case-in-chief, asserted the waiver defense and offered evidence demonstrating that the landlord told the tenant "Don't worry about paying your rent for the next year – you're my best buddy."

The landlord may, after the tenant's case-in-chief has concluded, present rebuttal evidence disputing this waiver defense. For example, the tenant had slipped the tea-totaling landlord a pint of grain alcohol in the landlord's non-alcoholic beer immediately before the landlord made this statement. Upon recovering from a massive hangover, the next day the landlord wrote the tenant a letter specifically disavowing "Any word, or portion thereof, coming out of my mouth" the night the alleged waiver was uttered.

E. RULES OF EVIDENCE

A party MUST be familiar with the rules of evidence which govern what the court will and will not consider as evidence.[133] A discussion of these rules is far beyond the scope of this guide; however, three *very oversimplified* evidentiary rules of thumb are:

- The evidence must be RELEVANT (relate to the subject at issue).[134]
- The testimonial evidence must be based on PERSONAL KNOWLEDGE,[135] documentary evidence must be through ORIGINAL or a DUPLICATE document.[136]
- Physical evidence (documents, photographs, objects) must be AUTHENTICATED (proven to be what they are purported to be).[137]

E.G.:

Most eviction actions involve a lease as evidence. This may be authenticated either through testimony of a witness who has personal knowledge that a document is what it is being claimed to be, or through identification of handwriting by a non-expert if this party is familiar with the handwriting and it was not acquired for the purpose of litigation. Typically, the

> party who signed the document is called to identify the document. Parties may also stipulate (agree) to authentification issues. This stipulation may either be in writing, before trial, or at the time of trial orally.

There are numerous exceptions and modifications of these rules as well as many other equally important rules. By no means should these rules of thumb be viewed as an alternative to familiarity with the Colorado Rules of Evidence.[138] A party preparing a case must keep these rules in mind. A party appearing at a hearing should also keep these rules in mind when objecting to testimony which does not comport with these requirements.

F. CLOSING ARGUMENTS

The closing argument's purpose is to comment upon the evidence which has been admitted, as well as reasonable inferences which may be drawn from the evidence. The parties should point out the strengths in their case, and point out the weakness of their opponent's case. The elements of the respective claims and defenses should be recapped with reference to the specific evidence (or lack thereof) presented on the particular points.

G. MOTION TO DISMISS

After the close of the plaintiff's direct evidence, the defendant may move for a dismissal of the case. A dismissal is appropriate if "upon the facts and the law the plaintiff has shown no right to relief."[139] Typically, a defendant will make this motion if the plaintiff failed to establish a crucial element of his/her case (e.g., no evidence presented regarding required pre-litigation notice; no evidence presented regarding alleged default). The court will then rule on this motion. If the court renders a judgment in favor of the defendant, the case is over and there is no need to go forward with any further evidence. If, however, the judge denies the motion, the defendant will then be entitled to present his/her case-in-chief.[140]

H. JUDGMENT

After all evidence has been received by the court, the court will enter a judgment on all claims, defenses and counterclaims. The rules specifically require that at the conclusion of a case, the court shall "forthwith orally announce its decision and direct the entry of the appropriate judgment."[141] No written findings are required.

1. Damages

The law provides that the prevailing party in an eviction action is entitled to damages that may include the following:

a. Damages "on account of unlawful detention of property" (i.e., past due rent)

b. Damages on account of injuries to the property (i.e., destruction of premises, legally known as "waste")

c. Court costs (i.e., clerk and sheriff fees)[142]

d. Reasonable attorneys' fees[143]

e. NOTE: THE DAMAGE TOTAL MAY NOT EXCEED THE JURISDICTIONAL LIMIT OF THE COURT ($10,000 for county courts)

2. Possession

At the time of judgment, a court may enter an order for immediate possession by the landlord. HOWEVER, THE COURT MAY NOT ISSUE A WRIT OF RESTITUTION UNTIL FORTY-EIGHT HOURS AFTER JUDGMENT IS ENTERED.

X. Writ of Restitution Procedure

The Writ of Restitution is the written document issued by the court to the sheriff directing the sheriff to physically remove the tenant and his/her personal property from the premises. A landlord should have this issued if the tenant has not voluntarily vacated the premises within forty-eight hours after the judgment has been entered.

A. WHEN WRIT ISSUED

A Writ of Restitution may not be issued until "after the expiration of forty-eight hours from the time of the entry of such judgment."[144] Nonetheless, the plaintiff should have the writ form completed and available for the court's review at the time of the judgment.

B. WHO ISSUES WRIT

Depending upon the jurisdiction, either the court will issue the writ or will authorize the clerk to issue it after the forty-eight hour period has passed. The specific mechanics of obtaining the writ vary by county. The general practice is to wait forty-eight hours and then request the issuance of a writ of restitution form from the clerk if the tenant has not vacated. In some jurisdictions, the court will issue the writ and postdate it by forty-eight hours. If you are uncertain about the local procedure, you may ask the judge or clerk.

C. WRIT OF RESTITUTION FORM (Form No. 538)

The law does not set forth specific requirements for the contents of this document. However, Colorado appears to have accepted the form available from Bradford Publishing Co. as the unofficial standard. *Exhibit W* is an example of this form.

EXHIBIT W

1 COURT, 2 COUNTY 3, COLORADO

Case No. 4 Div./CtRm 5

WRIT OF RESTITUTION

6 v.

Plaintiff(s) Defendant(s)

The People of the State of Colorado,
to the Sheriff of said County:

Whereas, 7 lately obtained

a judgment, against 8

in the above entitled action of *forcible entry, *forcible detainer or 9 *unlawful detainer, for the restitution of the premises following,

to wit:

10

and also for costs.

THESE ARE THEREFORE TO COMMAND YOU, in the name and by the authority of the People, to dispossess the said

11

and restore the said 12

to the possession of the said premises.

Hereof make due and proper return according to law.

Given under my hand and seal, this 13 day of ______________, 19 ____.

14
Clerk/Judge

By ______________________

*Strike according to fact.

No. 538. Rev. 11-86. WRIT OF RESTITUTION IN FORCIBLE ENTRY AND DETAINER
Bradford Publishing, 1743 Wazee St., Denver, CO 80202 — (303) 292-2500

D. FILLING OUT THE WRIT OF RESTITUTION (Form No. 538)

A completed Writ of Restitution form is included as *Exhibit X.*

Blank 1: "County" or "District" court

Blank 2: Leave blank unless in Denver; if in Denver, insert "City and"

Blank 3: Insert name of county

Blank 4: Insert case number

Blank 5: Insert court or division

Blank 6: Insert caption from Complaint

Blank 7: Insert plaintiff's name(s)

Blank 8: Insert defendant's name(s)

Line 9: Strike inapplicable language. In almost every action, "unlawful detainer" should be left and "forcible entry" and "forcible detainer" should be stricken.

Blank 10: Insert common and legal address, include unit or apartment number, if applicable.

Blank 11: Insert defendant's name(s)

Blank 12: Insert plaintiff's name(s)

Blank 13: Date issued; to be inserted by clerk or judge

Blank 14: Signature/seal of clerk or judge

EXHIBIT X

COUNTY COURT, CITY AND COUNTY OF DENVER, COLORADO
Case No. 95 C 1234 Div./CtRm 8

WRIT OF RESTITUTION

LOUISA L. LANDLORD
and
LENNY L. LANDLORD
Plaintiff(s)

v. THEODORE A. TENANT
Defendant(s)

The People of the State of Colorado,
to the Sheriff of said County:

Whereas, LOUISA L. AND LENNY L. LANDLORD ("Landlord") lately obtained a judgment, against THEODORE A. TENANT ("Tenant") on May 8, 1995 in the above entitled action of ~~*forcible entry, *forcible detainer or~~ *unlawful detainer, for the restitution of the premises following, to wit:

APARTMENT 7, 444 ST. JAMES PLACE, CITY AND COUNTY OF DENVER; LEGALLY DESCRIBED AS: LOT 6, BLOCK 2, JOHNSON'S ADDITION, 3rd FILING. COUNTY OF DENVER.

and also for costs.

THESE ARE THEREFORE TO COMMAND YOU, in the name and by the authority of the People, to dispossess the said THEODORE A. TENANT and restore the said LOUISA . LANDLORD and LENNY L. LANDLORD to the possession of the said premises.

Hereof make due and proper return according to law.

Given under my hand and seal, this 12th day of May, 19 95 .

Honorable Jon J. Judge
Clerk/Judge

By ______________________

*Strike according to fact.

No. 538. Rev. 11-86. WRIT OF RESTITUTION IN FORCIBLE ENTRY AND DETAINER
Bradford Publishing, 1743 Wazee St., Denver, CO 80202 — (303) 292-2500

E. SERVICE OF WRIT

Only the sheriff is authorized to serve the writ. It may only be served in the daytime, between "sunrise and sunset". The sheriff will charge an additional fee for service of the writ. The statute does not set forth the specific procedures which the sheriff must follow in acting upon the writ. Depending upon the county, some sheriffs will call or send a postcard prior to serving the writ. Finally, in some counties, the sheriff will serve the writ, wait for a period, and then return to physically dispossess the tenant if the tenant has not moved out. The sheriff of your county should be contacted to ascertain the specific procedures.

F. EXECUTION OF WRIT

The sheriff or deputy executing (carrying out) a writ is obliged to remove not only the tenant but also "to remove the tenant's personal property and effects from the premises." A landlord should be available at the time of the execution of the writ to allow access to the premises. HOWEVER, BEYOND LETTING THE AUTHORITIES IN, THE LANDLORD SHOULD DO NOTHING. DO NOT REMOVE THE PROPERTY. DO NOT MAKE EFFORTS TO STORE THE PROPERTY. Leave it to the sheriff. If the landlord follows this directive, he/she will not be liable for damages for the manner in which a sheriff executes the writ in the course of lawful eviction or removal of the tenant's property.

E.G.:

Counties handle the responsibility for actual removal of the property differently. Inquire as to the proper procedure. This may include the hiring of a third party moving company. In any event, follow the county's procedure precisely. Make sure the sheriff is supervising the actual removal.

An officer executing a writ is held only to a minimum standard of care. The officer must remove the tenant's property "without damaging it more than is necessary to execute the writ consistent with the natural consequences of removal."

Additionally, after removal, the officer has no duty to safeguard the tenant's possessions "even though he knows the tenant's belongings may be taken if they are left unattended." If a landlord participates in an eviction, or the landlord assumes possession or control of the property, the landlord may be held liable for loss or damage to the tenant's property. Therefore, the landlord is once again admonished not to do anything relating to the execution of the writ. Alternatively, if a tenant is faced with an overzealous landlord who has removed and/or damaged the tenant's possessions without proper authority or supervision by the sheriff, there is a good chance to recover against the landlord.

XI. Appeals

An eviction case tried in the county court may be appealed to the district court. The appeal will stay (stop) all further proceedings, including action in the writ of restitution while the appeal is pending. If an appeal is contemplated, an attorney familiar with the appeal process should be consulted at once. There are many deadline requirements, bonds and undertakings which must be complied with or the case will be thrown out.[145] The first of these deadlines is fifteen days from the date of the judgment. Therefore, timing and fast action are critical if an appeal is pursued. In addition to the regular appeal bond, a defendant appealing an eviction action must also deposit with the court the amount of money which was found due and owing as rent, plus additional rental payments as they become due during the pendency of the appeal.[146] Finally, an additional bond may be ordered by the court upon request of the appellee (non-appealing party) after a hearing.[147]

XII. Security Deposit Issues

A constant source of confusion with landlord and tenants is the status of security deposits in relation to evictions and the other aspects of the tenancy. A typical question is: Can a tenant use the security deposit as an offset against the last month's rent? Like almost all other landlord/tenant issues, the first place to look is the provisions of the particular lease involved. But usually the answer is "no." One major exception to this rule relates to the refund of security deposits at the end of a tenancy.

A. STATUTE: SECURITY DEPOSITS – WRONGFUL WITHHOLDING

The statute relating to the return of residential security deposits is definitely the most (and some say the only!) pro-tenant provision in the Colorado statutes. This statute sets forth requirements as to how a landlord must return security deposits to tenants and imposes severe penalties for failure to comply. This statute cannot be waived by oral or written agreement (e.g., in lease). The statute, § 38-12-103(1), C.R.S., is reprinted in Appendix D.

B. RETURN OF DEPOSIT

Within one month after the termination of a lease or surrender of the premises, the landlord is obliged to return to the tenant the security deposit. The lease may specify a longer period, but this period may not exceed sixty days.[148]

C. RETENTION OF SECURITY DEPOSIT/WRITTEN STATEMENT

If the landlord retains any portion of a security deposit, a written statement setting forth *the exact reasons* for the retention of said portion is required. This statement must be accompanied by a return of the balance of the deposit. *Exhibit Y* is an example of a written statement.

EXHIBIT Y

SECURITY DEPOSIT REFUND STATEMENT

TO:	Troy Tenant	Date:	April 15, 1995
	511 Grant Place	Commencement Date:	April 1, 1994
	Basement Unit	Security Deposit:	$500.00
	Empire, Colorado	Termination Date:	March 31, 1995

This statement is furnished to you pursuant to Section 38-12-103 of the Colorado Revised Statutes which governs the return of security deposits for residential premises. Enclosed is a check representing your security deposit minus deductions.

Credits:

Security Deposit: $500.00

Deductions:

Replacement of broken mirror: ($125.00)

1. Vanity mirror in bathroom

Mirror:	$75.00 at Milo's Mirror Mall
Labor:	$50.00; 2 hours @ $25.00/hour by Hank's Handymen

Replacement of kitchen knobs: ($10.00)

2. Missing kitchen cabinet knobs; replacement

Knobs:	$10.00; 10 @ $1.00/each
Labor:	NO CHARGE

3. Unpaid March, 1995 rent: ($250.00)

LESS TOTAL of ABOVE ITEMIZED REPAIRS/RENT: $385.00

TOTAL REFUND: $115.00

1. What May Be Deducted From Security Deposit

Absent a contrary provision in a lease, portions of the security deposit may be retained for:

a. Non-payment of rent;
b. Abandonment of the premises;
c. Non-payment of utility charges;
d. Repair work; or
e. Cleaning.[149]

A deduction may not be made from a security deposit for "normal wear and tear" of the premises.[150]

2. Delivery of Written Statement/Refund

The landlord is deemed to comply with the requirements of the statute if the landlord mails a statement and any required payment to the last known address of the tenant.

3. Effect of Failure to Deliver Written Statement

If landlord fails to comply with the above requirements and does not deliver a written statement and/or refund within the required time, the landlord *forfeits* all of the landlord's rights to withhold any portion of the security deposit. If the retention is "in willful violation" the landlord may be liable to the tenant for treble (three times) the amount of the security deposit wrongfully withheld plus attorneys' fees and court costs.

D. TENANT ACTION TO RECOVER SECURITY DEPOSIT

If a landlord is willfully retaining a security deposit, a tenant has the right to institute legal proceedings to recover same. A successful tenant may recover treble (three times) the amount of that portion of the security deposit wrongfully withheld, as well as costs and attorneys' fees. If a tenant contemplates an action against the landlord, it is imperative that the statutory requirements of a pre-litigation notice be complied with and further that the tenant be aware of the law as it relates to "wrongful withholding".

1. Pre-Litigation Notice

The law requires that a tenant give notice to the landlord of intent to file a legal proceeding prior to the filing of a security deposit action. This notice must be given at least seven (7) days prior to the filing of the action. It is suggested that this notice be sent via certified mail, return receipt requested, so there is proof that the landlord received the notice and that seven days have passed before the action is filed. An example of a pre-litigation notice appears in *Exhibit Z.*

EXHIBIT Z

TO: Lonnie Landlord
2147 West Ohio Street
Boulder, Colorado 80301

VIA CERTIFIED MAIL/RETURN RECEIPT REQUESTED
DELIVERY RESTRICTED TO ADDRESSEE ONLY

Date: March 15, 1995

NOTICE OF INTENT TO SUE

YOU ARE HEREBY NOTIFIED, pursuant to Colorado Revised Statutes Section 38-12-103(3)(a), that I, TOMMY TENANT, intend to file legal proceedings to recover the security deposit in the sum of Five Hundred and no/100 Dollars ($500.00) which is wrongfully withheld by you. The deposit was given to you in connection with my tenancy of the premises commonly known as 1330 Dearborn Street, Longmont, Colorado. This tenancy terminated on December 31, 1994. No written statement and/or refund has been received as of this date.

YOU ARE FURTHER NOTIFIED that said action will be filed on or after seven days from the date which you receive this Notice. This action will seek TREBLE THE AMOUNT OF THE DEPOSIT WHICH YOU CURRENTLY RETAIN, PLUS COSTS AND ATTORNEYS' FEES.

Signed,

Tommy Tenant

Tommy Tenant

2. SUIT TO RECOVER

Once the seven day period has expired, the tenant may file a lawsuit. Because attorneys' fees are recoverable, a tenant may consider consulting with an attorney and having the attorney file the case in county court.[151] However, if a tenant chooses to pursue the matter pro se, the small claims division of the county court is a simple and expeditious alternative.[152] Small claims courts have a jurisdictional limit of $5,000.00. This is subject to change and should be checked before filing. Generally, no attorneys may appear in small claims court. By law, the clerks for small claims court are required to provide assistance in the procedure of the court and are required to provide all necessary forms.[153] Note, however, that they cannot engage in the "practice of law". Service of process may be made by certified mail or personal service. A filing fee is also required. The return date set in small claims court will also be the trial date.

3. WILLFUL AND WRONGFUL WITHHOLDING

In order for a tenant to prevail against a landlord for treble damages, the court must find that the landlord's retention of the security deposit was both "willful" and "wrongful".[154]

a. Willful

"Willful retention" has been defined by the courts as "deliberate retention".[155] If a landlord deliberately fails to return a security deposit within the required seven day notice period, the retention is "logically willful under the act".

b. Wrongful

The landlord bears the burden of proof that withholding of the security deposit was not wrongful. Wrongful has been defined as acting in bad faith. One indication of a landlord's good faith is conformance with the written statement requirement when retaining a security deposit. On the other hand, if the landlord retains the security deposit and fails to provide the written statement, the withholding is presumed wrongful.[156]

4. Damages

A successful tenant in a wrongful security deposit retention action may recover treble (three times) damages. The calculation is based upon the amount retained, and not the entire amount of the security deposit. The tenant may also recover reasonable attorneys' fees and may recover costs of the suit. The costs of suit include filing fees and service of process fees.

E. SPECIAL PROVISION: GAS APPLIANCES

The legislature recently enacted new guidelines in regard to hazardous conditions of gas appliances. If a tenant is informed by a gas company service person of a hazardous condition, the tenant must immediately notify the landlord in writing. The landlord then has seventy-two hours to have the hazardous condition repaired. If the landlord fails to have the condition repaired, the tenant may vacate the premises and the lease becomes null and void. The tenant may then make a demand upon the landlord for immediate return of the security deposit. The landlord then has seventy-two hours in which to return the security deposit and/or written statement regarding any deposit retained and any rent abatement due. If this is not received by the tenant within the seventy-two hour period, the retention is deemed willful and wrongful, and the tenant is entitled to TWICE the amount of the deposit, plus attorneys' fees.[157] This seventy-two hour period excludes Saturdays, Sundays and Holidays.

F. CHECKLIST

The execution of pre-occupancy and post-occupancy checklists signed by both parties is one way which the parties to a lease may document the relative condition of the property. In the event a dispute subsequently arises, this checklist will serve as objective evidence as to the property's condition at a certain time. A checklist, Form 1133 Inspection Report, is available from Bradford Publishing.

XIII. Conclusion

Participating in an eviction, whether as a landlord, tenant or neophyte attorney, can be an emotional, anxious and mysterious experience. No matter how professionally the parties conduct themselves, emotions will always be present, because all litigants are human. Litigation is, by its very nature, unpredictable. This Guide attempts to give readers a better idea of what to expect and hopefully, this knowledge will serve to alleviate at least some of the mystery and anxiety during the eviction process.

Table of Appendices

APPENDIX A

Glossary of Legal Phrases and Abbreviations Used in Book

The legal profession employs a variety of phrases and abbreviations in its writings. While at first blush these might appear as devices intended to hide information, these phrases and abbreviations actually help to pinpoint and specify information. *Black's Law Dictionary,* 5th Edition, West Publishing Co. (1979) was consulted in connection with certain definitions. For more complete definitions, please see that text.

cf Compare; abbreviated from Latin "confer". When used in between two cases, it means compare these cases for similarities and differences.

Ibid., Id *In the same place.* When used in a footnote, it means that the information was derived from the book or source cited immediately above. Derived from the Latin word, Ibidness.

Supra *Before,* from the Latin prefix meaning upon above. When used in text, it refers to the information preceding.

Infra *After,* this is the opposite of "supra". When used in text, it means see the information following.

§ Symbol for "Section".

et seq. *The page referred to and following pages,* from the Latin "et sequetia".

E.g. *For example,* from the Latin word, "exempli gratia".

i.e. *That is to say. In other words,* from the Latin word "id est".

APPENDIX B

List of Eviction Forms Published By and Available From Bradford Publishing Co.

Form No. (use when ordering)	Title	Exhibit in this Guide
235PA	DEMAND FOR COMPLIANCE OR POSSESSION (also known as "3 DAY NOTICE")	A-E
219R	NOTICE TO QUIT (REPEAT VIOLATION OF COVENANT)	F-G
219S	NOTICE TO QUIT (SUBSTANTIAL VIOLATION)	H-I
219	NOTICE TO VACATE (also known as "10 DAY NOTICE"/ "NOTICE TO QUIT")	J-L
94	COMPLAINT	M-P
83	SUMMONS	Q&R
63	ANSWER	U&V
538	WRIT OF RESTITUTION	W&X

APPENDIX C

Colorado Revised Statutes

13-40-101. Forcible entry and detainer defined. (1) If any person enters upon or into any lands, tenements, mining claims, or other possessions with force or strong hand or multitude of people, whether any person is actually upon or in the same at the time of such entry, or if any person by threats of violence or injury to the party in possession or by such words or actions as have a natural tendency to excite fear or apprehension of danger gains possession of any lands, tenements, mining claims, or other possessions and detains and holds the same, such person so offending is guilty of a forcible entry and detainer within the meaning of this article.

(2) If any person enters peaceably upon any lands, tenements, mining claims, or other possessions, whether any person is actually in or upon the same at the time of such entry and by force turns the party in possession out or, by threats or by words or actions which have a natural tendency to excite fear or apprehension of danger, frightens the party out of possession and detains and holds the same, such person so offending is guilty of a forcible detainer within the meaning of this article.

(3) If any person enters upon or into any lands, tenements, mining claims, or other possessions by force or by threats of violence, or words or actions which have a natural tendency to excite fear or apprehension of danger, and intimidates the party entitled to possession from returning upon or possessing the same, such person so offending is guilty of a forcible entry within the meaning of this article.

13-40-102. Forcible entry prohibited. No person shall enter into or upon any real property, except in cases where entry is allowed by law, and in such cases not with strong hand or with a multitude of people, but only in a peaceable manner.

13-40-103. Forcible detention prohibited. No person, having peaceably entered into or upon any real property without right to the possession thereof, shall forcibly hold or detain the same as against the person who has a lawful right to such possession.

13-40-104. Unlawful detention defined. (1) Any person is guilty of an unlawful detention of real property in the following cases:

(a) When entry is made, without right or title, into any vacant or unoccupied lands or tenements;

(b) When entry is made, wrongfully, into any public lands, tenements, mining claims, or other possessions which are claimed or held by a person who may have located, entered, or settled upon the same in conformity with the laws, rules, and regulations of the United States, or of this state, in relation thereto;

(c) When any lessee or tenant at will, or by sufferance, or for any part of a year, or for one or more years, of any real property, including a specific or undivided portion of a building or dwelling, holds over and continues in possession of the demised premises, or any portion thereof, after the expiration of the term for which the same were leased, or after such tenancy, at will or sufferance, has been terminated by either party, except as provided in subsection (2) of this section;

(d) When such tenant or lessee holds over without permission of his landlord after any default in the payment of rent pursuant to the agreement under which he holds, and three days' notice in writing has been duly served upon the tenant or lessee holding over, requiring in the alternative the payment of the rent or the possession of the premises. No such agreement shall contain a waiver by the tenant of the three days' notice requirement of this paragraph (d). It shall not be necessary, in order to work a forfeiture of such agreement, for nonpayment of rent, to make a demand for such rent on the day on which the same becomes due; but a failure to pay such rent upon demand, when made, works a forfeiture.

(d.5) When such tenant or lessee holds over, without the permission of the landlord, contrary to any condition or covenant the violation of which is defined as a substantial violation in section 13-40-107.5, and notice in writing has been duly served upon such tenant or lessee in accordance with section 13-40-107.5;

(e) When such tenant or lessee holds over, without such permission, contrary to any other condition or covenant of the agreement under which such tenant or lessee holds, and three days' notice in writing has been duly served upon such tenant or lessee requiring in the alternative the compliance with such condition or covenant or the delivery of the possession of the premises so held.

(e.5) (I) When a tenant or lessee has previously been served with the notice described in paragraph (e) of this subsection (1) requiring compliance with a condition or covenant of the agreement, and subsequent to that notice holds over, without permission of the tenant or lessee's landlord, contrary to the same condition or covenant.

(II) A tenancy may be terminated at any time pursuant to this paragraph (e.5) on the basis of a subsequent violation. The termination shall be effective three days after service of written notice to quit.

(f) When the property has been duly sold under any power of sale, contained in any mortgage or trust deed which was executed by such person, or any person under whom he claims by title subsequent to date of the recording of such mortgage or trust deed, and the title under such sale has been duly perfected and the purchaser at such sale, or his assigns, has duly demanded the possession thereof, except as provided in subsection (2) of this section;

(g) When the property has been duly sold under the judgment or decree of any court of competent jurisdiction and the party or privies to such judgment or decree, after the expiration of the time of redemption when redemption is allowed by law, refuses or neglects to surrender possession thereof after demand therefor has been duly made by the purchaser at such sale, or his assigns, except as provided in subsection (2) of this section;

(h) When an heir or devisee continues in possession of any premises sold and conveyed by any personal representative with authority to sell, after demand therefor is duly made;

(i) When a vendee having obtained possession under an agreement to purchase lands or tenements, and having failed to comply with his agreement, withholds possession thereof from his vendor, or assigns, after demand therefor is duly made.

(2) Repealed.

(3) Repealed.

13-40-105. Crops of possessor. In all cases arising under section 13-40-104 (1) (c) to (1) (i), the person in possession is entitled to cultivate and gather the crops, if any, planted or sown by him previous to the service of the demand to deliver up possession, and then grown or growing on the premises, and shall have the right to enter such premises for the purpose of cultivating or removing such crops, first paying or tendering to the party entitled to the possession of said premises a reasonable compensation for the use of the land before removing such crops.

13-40-106. Written demand. The demand required by section 13-40-104 shall be made in writing, specifying the grounds of the demandant's right to the possession of such premises, describing the same, and the time when the same shall be delivered up, and shall be signed by the person claiming such possession, his agent, or his attorney.

13-40-107. Notice to quit. (1) A tenancy may be terminated by notice in writing, served not less than the respective period fixed before the end of the applicable tenancy, as follows:

(a) A tenancy for one year or longer, three months;

(b) A tenancy of six months or longer but less than a year, one month;

(c) A tenancy of one month or longer but less than six months, ten days;

(d) A tenancy of one week or longer but less than one month, or a tenancy at will, three days;

(e) A tenancy for less than one week, one day.

(2) Such notice shall describe the property and the particular time when the tenancy will terminate and shall be signed by the landlord or tenant, the party giving such notice or his agent or attorney.

(3) Any person in possession of real property with the assent of the owner is presumed to be a tenant at will until the contrary is shown.

(4) No notice to quit shall be necessary from or to a tenant whose term is, by agreement, to end at a time certain.

(5) Except as otherwise provided in section 38-33-112, C.R.S., the provisions of subsections (1) and (4) of this section shall not apply to the termination of a residential tenancy during the ninety-day period provided for in said section.

13-40-107.5. Termination of tenancy for substantial violation – definition – legislative declaration. (1) The general assembly finds and declares that:

(a) Violent and antisocial criminal acts are increasingly committed by persons who base their operations in rented homes, apartments, and commercial properties;

(b) Such persons often lease such property from owners who are unaware of the dangerous nature of such persons until after the persons have taken possession of the property;

(c) Under traditional landlord and tenant law, such persons may have established the technical, legal right to occupy the premises for a fixed term which continues long after they have demonstrated themselves unfit to coexist with their neighbors and co-tenants; furthermore, such persons often resist eviction as long as possible;

(d) In certain cases it is necessary to curtail the technical, legal right of occupancy of such persons in order to protect the equal or greater rights of neighbors and co-tenants, the interests of property owners, the values of trust and community within neighborhoods, and the health, safety, and welfare of all the people of this state.

(2) It is declared to be an implied term of every lease of real property in this state that the tenant shall not commit a substantial violation while in possession of the premises.

(3) As used in this section, "substantial violation" means any act or series of acts by the tenant or any guest or invitee of the tenant which, when considered together:

(a) Occurs on or near the premises and endangers the person or willfully and substantially endangers the property of the landlord, any co-tenant, or any person living on or near the premises; or

(b) Occurs on or near the premises and constitutes a violent or drug-related felony prohibited under article 3, 4, 6, 7, 9, 10, 12, or 18 of title 18, C.R.S.

(4) (a) A tenancy may be terminated at any time on the basis of a substantial violation. The termination shall be effective three days after service of written notice to quit.

(b) The notice to quit shall describe the property, the particular time when the tenancy will terminate, and the grounds for termination. The notice shall be signed by the landlord or by the landlord's agent or attorney.

(5) (a) In any action for possession under this section, the landlord has the burden of proving the occurrence of a substantial violation by a preponderance of the evidence.

(b) In any action for possession under this section, it shall be a defense that:

(I) The tenant is a victim of domestic violence that has been documented by the filing of a police report or the issuance of a restraining order and the domestic violence is the basis for the termination notice; or

(II) The tenant did not know of, and could not reasonably have known of or prevented, the commission of a substantial violation by a guest or invitee but immediately notified a law enforcement officer of his knowledge of the substantial violation.

13-40-108. Service of notice to quit. A notice to quit or demand for possession of real property may be served by delivering a copy thereof to the tenant or other person occupying such premises, or by leaving such copy with some person, a member of the tenant's family above the age of fifteen years, residing on or in charge of the premises, or, in case no one is on the premises at the time service is attempted, by posting such copy in some conspicuous place on the premises.

13-40-109. Jurisdiction of courts. The district courts in their respective districts and county courts in their respective counties have jurisdiction of all cases of forcible entry, forcible detainer, or unlawful detainer arising under this article, and the person entitled to the possession of any premises may recover possession thereof by action brought in any of said courts in the manner provided in this article. On and after January 1, 1991, in all actions brought before county courts under section 13-40-104 (1) (f) to (1) (i), where the allegations of the complaint are put in issue by a verified answer and in actions in which the verified answer alleges a monthly rental value of the property in excess of ten thousand dollars, the county court, upon the filing of said answer, shall suspend all proceedings therein and certify said cause and transmit the papers therein to the district court of the same county. Causes so certified by the county court shall be proceeded within the courts to which they have been so certified in all respects as if originally begun in the court to which they have been certified. On and after January 1, 1991, the jurisdiction of the county court to enter judgment for rent, or damages, or both and to render judgment on a counterclaim in forcible entry and detainer shall be limited to a total of ten thousand dollars in favor of either party, exclusive of costs and attorney fees.

13-40-110. Action – how commenced. (1) An action under this article is commenced by filing with the court a complaint in writing describing the property with reasonable certainty, the grounds for the recovery thereof, the name of the person in possession or occupancy, and a prayer for recovery of possession. The complaint may also set forth the amount of rent due, the rate at which it is accruing, the amount of damages due, and the rate at which they are accruing and may include a prayer for rent due or to become due, present and future damages, costs, and any other relief to which plaintiff is entitled.

(2) In an action for termination of a tenancy in a mobile home park, the complaint, in addition to the requirements of subsection (1) of this section, shall specify the particular reasons for termination as such reasons are stated in section 38-12-203, C.R.S. Such complaint shall specify the approximate time, place, and manner in which the tenant allegedly committed the acts giving rise to the complaint.

13-40-111. Issuance and return of summons. Upon filing the complaint as provided in section 13-40-110, the clerk of the court or the attorney for the plaintiff shall issue a summons. The summons shall command the defendant to appear before the court at a place named in such summons and at a time and on a day which shall be not less than five days nor more than ten days from the day of issuing the same to answer the complaint of plaintiff. The summons shall also contain a statement addressed to the defendant stating: "If you fail to file with the court, at or before the time for appearance specified in the summons, an answer to the complaint setting forth the grounds upon which you base your claim for possession and denying or admitting all of the material allegations of the complaint, judgment by default may be taken against you for the possession of the property described in the complaint, for the rent, if any, due or to become due, for present and future damages and costs, and for any other relief to which the plaintiff is entitled.".

13-40-112. Service. (1) Such summons may be served by personal service as in any civil action. A copy of the complaint must be served with the summons.

(2) If personal service cannot be had upon the defendant by a person qualified under the Colorado rules of civil

procedure to serve process, after having made diligent effort to make such personal service, such person may make service by posting a copy of the summons and the complaint in some conspicuous place upon the premises. In addition thereto, the plaintiff shall mail, no later than the next day following the day on which he files the complaint, a copy of the summons, or, in the event that an alias summons is issued, a copy of the alias summons, and a copy of the complaint to the defendant at the premises by postage prepaid, first-class mail.

(3) Personal service or service by posting shall be made at least five days before the day for appearance specified in such summons, and the time and manner of such service shall be endorsed upon such summons by the person making service thereof.

13-40-113. Answer of defendant – additional and amended pleadings. (1) The defendant shall file with the court, at or before the time specified for his appearance in the summons, an answer in writing setting forth the grounds on which he bases his claim for possession and admitting or denying all of the material allegations of the complaint and presenting every defense which then exists and upon which he intends to rely, either by including the same in his answer or by filing simultaneously therewith motions setting forth every such defense.

(2) The court for good cause may permit the filing of additional and amended pleadings where such will not result in delay prejudicial to the defendant.

13-40-114. Delay in trial – undertaking. If either party requests a delay in trial longer than five days, the court in its discretion may, upon good cause shown, require either of the parties to give bond or other security approved and fixed by the court in an amount for the payment to the opposite party of such sum as he may be damaged due to the delay.

13-40-115. Judgment – writ of restitution. (1) Upon the trial of any action under this article if service was had only by posting in accordance with section 13-40-112 (2) and if the court finds that the defendant has committed an unlawful detainer, the court shall enter judgment for the plaintiff to have restitution of the premises and shall issue a writ of restitution. The court may also continue the case for further hearing from time to time and may issue alias and pluries summonses until personal service upon the defendant is had.

(2) Upon such trial or further hearing under this article after personal service is had upon the defendant in accordance with section 13-40-112 (1), if the court or jury has not already tried the issue of unlawful detainer, it may do so, and, if it finds that the defendant has committed an unlawful detainer, the court shall enter judgment for the plaintiff to have restitution of the premises and shall issue a writ of restitution. In addition to such judgment for restitution, the court or jury shall further find the amount of rent, if any, due to the plaintiff from the defendant at the time of trial, the amount of damages, if any, sustained by the plaintiff to the time of the trial on account of the unlawful detention of the property by the defendant, and damages sustained by the plaintiff to the time of trial on account of injuries to the property, and judgment shall enter for such amounts, together with reasonable attorney's fees and costs, upon which judgment execution shall issue as in other civil actions. Nothing in this section shall be construed to permit the entry of judgment in excess of the jurisdictional limit of the court.

APPENDIX D

Colorado Revised Statutes

38-12-101. Legislative declaration. The provisions of this part 1 shall be liberally construed to implement the intent of the general assembly to insure the proper administration of security deposits and protect the interests of tenants and landlords.

38-12-102. Definitions. As used in this part 1, unless the context otherwise requires:

(1) "Normal wear and tear" means that deterioration which occurs, based upon the use for which the rental unit is intended, without negligence, carelessness, accident, or abuse of the premises or equipment or chattels by the tenant or members of his household, or their invitees or guests.

(2) "Security deposit" means any advance or deposit of money, regardless of its denomination, the primary function of which is to secure the performance of a rental agreement for residential premises or any part thereof.

38-12-103. Return of security deposit. (1) A landlord shall, within one month after the termination of a lease or surrender and acceptance of the premises, whichever occurs last, return to the tenant the full security deposit deposited with the landlord by the tenant, unless the lease agreement specifies a longer period of time, but not to exceed sixty days. No security deposit shall be retained to cover normal wear and tear. In the event that actual cause exists for retaining any portion of the security deposit, the landlord shall provide the tenant with a written statement listing the exact reasons for the retention of any portion of the security deposit. When the statement is delivered, it shall be accompanied by payment of the difference between any sum deposited and the amount retained. The landlord is deemed to have complied with this section by mailing said statement and any payment required to the last known address of the tenant. Nothing in this section shall preclude the landlord from retaining the security deposit for nonpayment of rent, abandonment of the premises, or nonpayment of utility charges, repair work, or cleaning contracted for by the tenant.

(2) The failure of a landlord to provide a written statement within the required time specified in subsection (1) of this

section shall work a forfeiture of all his rights to withhold any portion of the security deposit under this section.

(3) (a) The willful retention of a security deposit in violation of this section shall render a landlord liable for treble the amount of that portion of the security deposit wrongfully withheld from the tenant, together with reasonable attorneys' fees and court costs; except that the tenant has the obligation to give notice to the landlord of his intention to file legal proceedings a minimum of seven days prior to filing said action.

(b) In any court action brought by a tenant under this section, the landlord shall bear the burden of proving that his withholding of the security deposit or any portion of it was not wrongful.

(4) Upon cessation of his interest in the dwelling unit, whether by sale, assignment, death, appointment of a receiver, or otherwise, the person in possession of the security deposit, including but not limited to the landlord, his agent, or his executor, shall, within a reasonable time:

(a) Transfer the funds, or any remainder after lawful deductions under subsection (1) of this section, to the landlord's successor in interest and notify the tenant by mail of such transfer and of the transferee's name and address; or

(b) Return the funds, or any remainder after lawful deductions under subsection (1) of this section, to the tenant.

(5) Upon compliance with subsection (4) of this section, the person in possession of the security deposit shall be relieved of further liability.

(6) Upon receipt of transferred funds under subsection (4) (a) of this section, the transferee, in relation to such funds, shall be deemed to have all of the rights and obligations of a landlord holding the funds as a security deposit.

(7) Any provision, whether oral or written, in or pertaining to a rental agreement whereby any provision of this section for the benefit of a tenant or members of his household is waived shall be deemed to be against public policy and shall be void.

38-12-104. Return of security deposit - hazardous condition – gas appliance. (1) Anytime service personnel from any organization providing gas service to a residential building become aware of any hazardous condition of a gas appliance, piping, or other gas equipment, such personnel shall inform the customer of record at the affected address in writing of the hazardous condition and take any further action provided for by the policies of such personnel's employer. Such written notification shall state the potential nature of the hazard as a fire hazard or a hazard to life, health, property, or public welfare and shall explain the possible cause of the hazard.

(2) If the resident of the residential building is a tenant, such tenant shall immediately inform the landlord of the property or the landlord's agent in writing of the existence of the hazard.

(3) The landlord shall then have seventy-two hours excluding a Saturday, Sunday, or a legal holiday after the actual receipt of the written notice of the hazardous condition to have the hazardous condition repaired by a professional. "Professional" for the purposes of this section means a person authorized by the state of Colorado or by a county or municipal government through license or certificate where such government authorization is required. Where no person with such government authorization is available, and where there are no local requirements for government authorization, a person who is otherwise qualified and who possesses insurance with a minimum of one hundred thousand dollars public liability and property damage coverage shall be deemed a professional for purposes of this section. Proof of such repairs shall be forwarded to the landlord or the landlord's agent. Such proof may also be used as an affirmative defense in any action to recover the security deposit, as provided for in this section.

(4) If the landlord does not have the repairs made within seventy-two hours excluding a Saturday, Sunday, or a legal holiday, and the condition of the building remains hazardous, the tenant may opt to vacate the premises. After the tenant vacates the premises, the lease or other rental agreement between the landlord and tenant becomes null and void, all rights and future obligations between the landlord and tenant pursuant to the lease or other rental agreement terminate, and the tenant may demand the immediate return of all or any portion of the security deposit held by the landlord to which the tenant is entitled. The landlord shall have seventy-two hours following the tenant's vacation of the premises to deliver to the tenant all of, or the appropriate portion of, the security deposit plus any rent rebate owed to the tenant for rent paid by the tenant for

the period of time after the tenant has vacated. If the seventy-second hour falls on a Saturday, Sunday, or legal holiday, the security deposit must be delivered by noon on the next day that is not a Saturday, Sunday, or legal holiday. The tenant shall provide the landlord with a correct forwarding address. No security deposit shall be retained to cover normal wear and tear. In the event that actual cause exists for retaining any portion of the security deposit, the landlord shall provide the tenant with a written statement listing the exact reasons for the retention of any portion of the security deposit. When the statement is delivered, it shall be accompanied by payment of the difference between any sum deposited and the amount retained. The landlord is deemed to have complied with this section by mailing said statement and any payments required by this section to the forwarding address of the tenant. Nothing in this section shall preclude the landlord from withholding the security deposit for nonpayment of rent or for nonpayment of utility charges, repair work, or cleaning contracted for by the tenant. If the tenant does not receive the entire security deposit or a portion of the security deposit together with a written statement listing the exact reasons for the retention of any portion of the security deposit within the time period provided for in this section, the retention of the security deposit shall be deemed willful and wrongful and, notwithstanding the provisions of section 38-12-103 (3), shall entitle the tenant to twice the amount of the security deposit and to reasonable attorney fees.

RULE 4, C.R.C.P. PROCESS

(a) To What Applicable. This Rule applies to all process except as otherwise provided by these rules.

(b) Issuance of Summons by Attorney or Clerk. The summons may be signed and issued by the clerk, under the seal of the court, or it may be signed and issued by the attorney for the plaintiff. Separate additional or amended summons may issue against any defendant at any time. All other process shall be issued by the clerk, except as otherwise provided in these rules.

(c) Contents of Summons. The summons shall contain the name of the court, the county in which the action is brought, the names or designation of the parties, shall be directed to the defendant, shall state the time within which the defendant is required to appear and defend against the claims of the complaint, and shall notify him that in case of his failure to do so, judgment by default may be rendered against him. If the summons is served by publication, the summons shall briefly state the sum of money or other relief demanded. The summons shall in the signature element thereof, contain the name, address, and registration number of the plaintiff's attorney, if any, and if not, the address of the plaintiff. Except in case of service by publication under Rule 4 (h) or when otherwise ordered by the court, the complaint shall be served with the summons, and in all other cases service of a summons alone after the effective date of this amended rule shall not constitute service of process. In any case, where by special order personal service of summons is allowed without the complaint, a copy of the order shall be served with the summons.

(d) By Whom Served. Process may be served:

(1) Within the state, by the sheriff of the county where the service is made, or by his deputy, or by any other person over the age of eighteen years, not a party to the action;

(2) At any other place by a sheriff, deputy sheriff, constable, deputy constable, bailiff, deputy bailiff, or other officer having like powers and duties of the political subdivision in which the service is made or an officer authorized by the laws of this state to take acknowledgements in such political subdivision to deeds conveying real estate situate in this state or an attorney, counselor at law, solicitor, advocate, barrister duly qualified to practice law in such political subdivision or a person specially commissioned to serve process by the court in which the action is pending.

(e) Personal Service in State. Personal service within the state shall be as follows:

(I) Upon a natural person over the age of eighteen years by delivering a copy or copies thereof to him personally, or by leaving a copy or copies thereof at his dwelling house or usual place of abode, with some member of his family over the age of eighteen years, or at his usual place of business, with his stenographer, bookkeeper, or chief clerk; or by delivering a copy to an agent authorized by appointment or by law to receive service of process;

(2) Upon a natural person, between the ages of thirteen years and eighteen years, by delivering a copy thereof to such person and another copy thereof to his father, mother, or guardian, or if there be none in the state, then by delivering a copy thereof to any person in whose care or control he may be; or with whom he resides, or in whose service he is employed; and upon a natural person under the age of thirteen years by delivering a copy to his father, mother, or guardian;

(3) Upon a person for whom a conservator has been appointed, by delivering a copy thereof to such conservator;

(4) Upon a partnership, or other unincorporated association, by delivering a copy thereof to one or more of the partners or associates, or a managing or general agent thereof;

(5) Upon a private corporation, by delivering a copy thereof to any officer, manager, general agent, or registered agent. If no such officer or agent can be found in the county in which the action is brought, such copy may be delivered to any stockholder, agent, member, or principal employee found in such county. If such service is upon a person other than an executive officer, the secretary, general agent, or registered agent, then the clerk shall mail a copy thereof to the corporation at its last known address, at least twenty days before default is entered;

(6) Upon a municipal corporation, by delivering a copy thereof to the mayor or clerk or deputy clerk of such corporation;

(7) Upon a county, by delivering a copy thereof to the county clerk or his chief deputy;

(8) Upon a school district, by delivering a copy thereof to the clerk or one of the directors of such school district;

(9) Upon the state by delivering a copy thereof to the attorney general, or to any employee in his office designated by him to accept service of process;

(10) (A) Upon an officer, agent, or employee of the state, acting in his official capacity, by delivering a copy thereof to the officer, agent, or employee, and by delivering a copy to the attorney general, or to any employee in his office designated by him to accept service of process.

(B) Upon a department or agency of the state, subject to suit, by delivering a copy thereof to the principal officer, chief clerk, or other executive employee thereof, and by delivering a copy to the attorney general, or any employee in his office designated by him to accept service of process.

(C) For all purposes the date of service upon the officer, agent, employee, department, or agency shall control, except that failure to serve copies upon the attorney general within three days of service upon the officer, agent, employee, department, or agency shall extend the time within which the officer, agent, employee, department, or agency must file a responsive pleading for sixty days beyond the time otherwise provided by these Rules.

(f) Personal Service Outside the State. Personal service outside the state may be made:

(I) In any action, upon a natural person over the age of eighteen years who is a resident of this state, or who is a nonresident of this state and who has submitted to or has become subject by law to the jurisdiction of the courts of this state, by delivering a copy of the process, together with a copy of the pleading upon which it was issued, to the person served;

(2) In any action, upon a person other than a natural person, who is either domiciled in this state or is domiciled in another state and who has submitted to or has become subject by law to the jurisdiction of the courts of this state, by delivering a copy of the process, together with a copy of the pleading upon which it was issued, in the manner provided by this Rule for personal service in this state upon such person;

(3) In any action affecting specific property or status or in any other proceeding in rem, upon a natural person of any age, without regard to his residence, or upon any other person, without regard to his domicile, by delivering a copy of the pleading and process thereon, in the manner provided by this Rule for personal service in this state upon such person. Service under this section (3) upon a natural person, between the ages of thirteen years and eighteen years, by delivering a copy of said pleading and process to such person and another copy thereof to his father, mother, or guardian, or if there be none in that state, then by delivering a copy thereof to any person in whose care or control he may be, or with whom he resides, or in whose service he is employed, and upon a natural person under the age of thirteen years by delivering a copy to his father, mother, or guardian, wherever, within or without this state, such person may be found;

(4) No provision of this section (f) shall be construed to limit the right to serve process in any other manner authorized by this Rule.

(g) Other Service. Service by mail or publication shall be allowed only in cases affecting specific property or status or other proceedings in rem.

(1) If the person to be served is without the state of Colorado, the party desiring service by mail shall file a motion verified by the oath of such party or of someone in his behalf for an order for service by mail. Such motion shall state the facts showing why such method of service is advisable, and the address of the person to be served. The court may, after hearing the motion ex parte, direct the clerk to send by registered or certified mail a copy of the process and a copy of the complaint, addressed to such person at such address, requesting a return receipt signed by addressee only. Such service shall be complete on the date of the filing of the clerk's proof thereof, together with such return receipt attached thereto signed by such addressee.

(2) Service by publication may be had on the following parties:

(A) Unknown persons;

(B) Domestic corporations. When such corporation cannot be served because no person can be found upon whom such service can be made;

(C) Foreign corporations. When such corporation has not appointed a registered agent, or when the registered agent appointed cannot be found at the registered office;

(D) Nonresidents of the state; persons who have departed from the state without intention of returning; persons who conceal themselves to avoid service of process; or persons whose whereabouts are unknown and who cannot be served by personal service in the state.

(h) Publication. The party desiring service of process by publication shall file a motion verified by the oath of such party or of someone in his behalf for an order of publication. It shall state the facts authorizing such service, and shall show the efforts, if any, that have been made to obtain personal service within this state and shall give the address, or last known address, of each person to be served or shall state that his address and last known address are unknown. The court shall hear the motion ex parte and, if satisfied that due diligence has been used to obtain personal service within this state or that efforts to obtain the same would have been to no avail, shall order publication of the process in a newspaper published in the county in which the action is pending. Such publication shall be made for four weeks. Within fifteen days after the order the clerk shall mail a copy of the process to each person whose address or last known address has been stated in the motion. Service shall be complete on the day of the last publication. If no newspaper is published in the county, the court shall designate one in some adjoining county.

(i) Manner of Proof.

(1) If served in a state or territory of the United States by a sheriff or his deputy, by his certificate with a statement as to date, place, and manner of service;

(2) If by any other person, by his affidavit thereof, with the same statement;

(3) If by mail, by the certificate of the clerk showing the date of the mailing, and the date he received the return receipt;

(4) If by publication, by the affidavit of publication, together with the certificate of the clerk as to the mailing of copy of the process where required;

(5) By the written admission or waiver of service by the person or persons to be served, duly acknowledged.

(j) Amendment. At any time in its discretion and upon such terms as it deems just, the court may allow any process or proof of service thereof to be amended, unless it clearly appears that material prejudice would result to the substantial rights of the party against whom the process is issued.

(k) Refusal of Copy. If the person to be served refuses to accept a copy of the process, service shall be sufficient if the person serving the same shall state the name of the process and offer to deliver a copy thereof.

RULE 304, C.R.C.P. SERVICE OF PROCESS

(a) To What Applicable. Except as otherwise provided by these rules, all process shall be served in the same manner as service of a summons and complaint.

(b) Initial Process. Except in cases of service by publication under Rule 304(e), the complaint and a blank copy of the answer form shall be served with the summons, and in all other cases service of a summons alone after the effective date of this amended rule shall not constitute service of process.

(c) By Whom Served. The summons and complaint may be served inside or outside this state, by the sheriff of the county where the service is made, or by the sheriff's deputy, or by any other person over the age of eighteen years, not a party to the action.

(d) Personal Service. Personal service of the summons and complaint shall be as follows:

(1) Upon a natural person over the age of eighteen years, by delivering a copy thereof to the person, or leaving a copy at the person's usual place of abode, with any person over the age of eighteen years who is a member of the person's family, or at the person's usual place of business, with the person's secretary, bookkeeper, or chief clerk; or by delivering a copy to an agent authorized by appointment or by law to receive service of process.

(2) Upon a natural person under the age of eighteen years, by delivering a copy thereof to the person and a copy thereof to the person's father, mother, or guardian, or if there be none in the state, then by delivering a copy thereof to any person in whose care or control the person may be, or with whom the person resides, or in whose service the person is employed.

(3) Upon a person for whom a conservator has been appointed, by delivering a copy thereof to such conservator.

(4) Upon a partnership, or other unincorporated association, by delivering a copy thereof to one or more of the partners or associates, or a managing or general agent thereof.

(5) Upon a private corporation, by delivering a copy thereof to any officer, manager, general agent, or agent for process. If no such office or agent can be found in the county in which the action is brought, such copy may be delivered to any stockholder, agent, member or principal employee found in such county. If such service be upon a person other than an executive officer, the secretary, general agent, or agent for process, then the clerk shall mail a copy thereof to the corporation at its last known address, at least fifteen days before default is entered.

(6) Upon a municipal corporation, by delivering a copy thereof to the mayor or clerk of such corporation.

(7) Upon a county, by delivering a copy thereof to the county clerk and recorder or chief deputy.

(8) Upon a school district, by delivering a copy thereof to the clerk or one of the directors of such school district.

(9) Upon a department or agency of the state, subject to suit, by delivering a copy thereof to the principal officer, chief clerk, or other executive employee thereof.

(e) Other Service. Service by mail or publication shall be allowed only in actions affecting specific property or status or other proceedings in rem. When service is by publication, the complaint need not be published with the summons. The party desiring service of process by mail or publication shall file a motion verified by the oath of such party or of someone in the party's behalf for an order of service by mail or publication. It shall state the facts authorizing such service, and shall show the efforts, if any, that have been made to obtain personal service and shall give the address, or last known address, of each person to be served or shall state that this address and last known address are unknown. The court shall hear the motion ex parte and, if satisfied that due diligence has been used to obtain personal service or that efforts to obtain the same would have been to no avail, shall:

(1) Order the clerk to send by registered or certified mail a copy of the summons and a copy of the complaint, addressed to such person at such address, requesting a return receipt signed by addressee only. Such service shall be complete on the date of the filing of the clerk's proof thereof, together with such return receipt attached thereto signed by such addressee, or

(2) Order publication of the summons in a newspaper published in the county in which the action is pending. Such publication shall be made for four weeks. Within fifteen days after the order the clerk shall mail a copy of the summons and complaint to each person whose address or last known address has been stated in the motion. Service shall be completed on the day of the last publication. If no newspaper be published in the county, the court shall designate one in some adjoining county.

(f) Manner of Proof.

(1) If served in a state or territory of the United States by a sheriff or United States marshal, or a deputy, by such person's certificate with a statement as to date, place and manner of service.

(2) If by any other person, by the person's affidavit thereof, with the same statement.

(3) If by mail, by the certificate of the clerk showing the date of the mailing, and the date the clerk received the return receipt.

(4) If by publication, by the affidavit of publication, together with the certificate of the clerk as to the mailing of copy of the summons where required.

(5) By the written admission or waiver of service by the person to be served, duly acknowledged.

(g) Amendment. At any time in its discretion and upon such terms as it deems just, the court may allow any summons or proof of service thereof to be amended, unless it clearly appears that material prejudice would result to the substantial rights of the party against whom the summons issued.

(h) Refusal of Copy. If a person to be served refuses to accept a copy of the summons and complaint, service shall be sufficient if the person serving the documents knows or has reason to identify the person who refuses to be served, identifies the documents being served as a summons and complaint, and offers to deliver a copy of the documents to the person who refuses to be served.

APPENDIX E

A Directory of Professionals in Alternative Dispute Resolutions is available by calling the Colorado Council of Mediators or the Colorado Bar Association.

Colorado Council of Mediators & Mediation Organizations
1660 Lincoln Street, #2150
Denver, CO 80264
(303) 322-9275 (800) 864-4317

Colorado Bar Association
1900 Grant Street, Suite 950
Denver, CO 80203
(303) 860-1115

Office of Dispute Resolution
Colorado Judicial Department
1301 Pennsylvania, #300
Denver, CO 80203
(303) 837-3672 (303) 861-1111

Office of Dispute Resolution
Colorado Judicial Department
20 E. Vermijo
Colorado Springs, CO 80903
(719) 630-2948

Office of Dispute Resolution
Colorado Judicial Department
P.O. Box 251
Grand Junction, CO 81502
(303) 243-9134

Office of Dispute Resolution
Colorado Judicial Department
P.O. Box 773117
Steamboat Springs, CO 80477
(303) 879-5020

Judicial Arbiter Group, Inc.
1601 Blake Street, #400
Denver, CO 80202
(303) 572-1919

Endnotes

Legal citations to cases, statutory law and articles contained in the endnotes use the following abbreviations:

C.R.S. – Colorado Revised Statutes

C.R.C.P. – Colorado Rules of Civil Procedure

P. 2nd – refers to citations from Pacific Care Reporter, 2nd Edition, West Publishing

Colo. Law – Colorado Lawyer Magazine, published by the Colorado Bar Association

Denv. U.L.J. – Denver University Law Journal

U.S. – United States Supreme Court

1 C. Koenigs, *Enforcement of Leases Through Unlawful Detainer Actions,* 20 Colo. Law 251, 252 (Feb. 1991). Hereinafter "Koenigs".

2 Deeb v. Canniff, 488 P. 2d 93 (Colo. App. 1971) (Conversion); Montgomery v. Tufford, 437 P. 2d 36 (Colo. 1968) (Trespass and Conversion); Danyew v. Phelps, 676 P. 2d 707 (Colo. App. 1983) (Outrageous conduct).

3 See e.g. Clark v. Morris, 710 P. 2d 1130 (Colo. App. 1985), Montgomery v. Tufford, supra.

4 E.g., "Landlord may, at his option, without liability for trespass or for damages, enter into and upon said premises...repossess the said premises...expel and remove the tenant...and their effects...all without prejudice to any other remedies available to the landlord for arrears of rent or breach of covenant." Bradford Publishing Co.; Apartment Lease, Form No. 1045.

5 See e.g., Clark v. Morris, 710 P. 2d 1130 (Colo. App. 1985) (Implying that if landlord complies with specific provisions of lease self help would be okay). cf Manuel A. Ramos, *Rights and Obligations: Colorado Landlord-Tenant Law from the Prospective of a Tenant Advocate,* pp. 5-7 (1992). Hereinafter "Ramos". ("Landlord `Self-Help' has not been condoned by Colorado courts", p. 33); D. Cypser, "Survey of Colorado Landlord and Tenant Law," 20 Colo. Law 2023 (Oct. 1991), hereinafter "Cypser" ("However, recent cases have held that an unlawful detainer action and a writ of restitution executed by an officer of the law are the only lawful means of evicting a tenant. Lockouts and other `self-help' evictions are not lawful." at 2026). See also Koenigs, supra at note 1, p. 252; D. Rubin, "Representation of the Landlord in an Unlawful Detainer Action," 12 Colo. Law 69, 72 (Oct. 1983) (hereinafter "Rubin"). Both cautioning against self-help actions.

6 E.g., "In the event the premises are left vacant...then landlord may...retake possession of said premises..." Bradford Publishing; Apartment Lease, Form No. 1045.

7 Ruston v. Centennial Real Estate and Investment, 445 P. 2d 64 (1968); Martinez v. Steinbaum, 623 P. 2d 49 (Colo. 1981).

8 See Martinez, supra, (Holding that tenant reporting he would be back in two to three days and not returning for eight weeks had abandoned the property); cf Berae Company v. Gorman, 452 P. 2d 379 (Colo. 1969), (Meat market closed for ten days, not abandoned).

9 See e.g. Clark v. Morris, 710 P. 2d 1130 (Colo. App. 1985).

10 Martinez v. Steinbaum, 623 P. 2d 49, 53 (Colo. 1981); Berae Company v. Gorman, 452 P. 2d 379 (Colo. 1969).

11 Berae, supra at 380

12 Berae Company v. Gorman, 452 P.2d 379 (Colo. 1969); See also Deeb v. Canniff; 488 P.2d 93 (Colo. App. 1971).

13 Martinez v. Steinbaum, 623 P.2d 49 (Colo. 1981); See also Ruston v. Centennial Real Estate Improvements, 445 P.2d 64 (Colo. 1966).

14 Rubin, supra, Note 5 at 72. "It is preferable to get the judgment...in order to avoid any doubt as to the legality of the actions by the landlord. Often in an effort to save time and costs the landlord places himself in a more precarious position than before".

15 § 38-20-101 et seq. C.R.S. (This applies to residential premises); See generally, J. Gigax, Rights of Landlords in Tenant's Personal Property, 57 Denv. U.L.J. 685 (1980) (hereinafter "Gigax"). See also Senn and Jones, Self Help for Commercial Landlords, 19, Colo. Law 479 (March 1990).

16 § 38-20-102(3)(c) C.R.S. Assertion of lien in a forcible manner or manner than interferes with tenant's right of occupancy is wrongful.

17 Gigax, supra, at Note 15 at 693; M. Ramos, "Colorado's Landlord Lien Statute: Equal Protection and Due Process Infirmities," 11 Colo. Law. 1867 (July 1982)

18 § 13-40-104(d) C.R.S.

19 The designation of "Demand for Possession" is actually misleading because the landlord is more properly giving the tenant a "notice to pay or quit". See Barlow v. Hoffman, 86 P. 2d 239, 241, 103 Colo. 286, 291 (Colo. 1938). Aigner v. Lowell Sales Company, 660 P. 2d 907, 908 (Colo. 1983), GTM Investments v. The Depot, Inc., 694 P. 2d 379, 382 (Colo. App. 1984). This guide will refer to this document as a "Demand for Compliance or Possession" because this is what the form employed is entitled.

20 § 13-40-104(e) C.R.S.

21 § 13-40-104(e.5) C.R.S. Effective July 1, 1995)

22 § 13-40-107.5 C.R.S. and §13-40-104 (d.5)

23 Francam Building Corporation v. Fail, 646 P. 2d 345 (Colo. 1982).

24 § 13-40-104(d) C.R.S. "No such agreement shall contain a waiver by the tenant of a three day notice requirement of this paragraph (d)".

25 Note, however, the above language applies only to the non-payment of rent defaults under paragraph (d) and is not referenced to paragraph (e) which relates to "any other condition or covenant". Query: Does this mean Francam is still good law as applied to notice requirement in (e)? This question is unanswered by case law or the legislature. The more conservative approach would be to serve a defaulting tenant a 3 Day Notice even if a default is under paragraph (e) and the lease contains a waiver. This will assure that the case will not be thrown out under a misreading of Section 13-40-104(d)/(e).

26 § 13-40-104(d) C.R.S.

27 § 13-40-104(d) C.R.S. It must be addressed to all tenants on the property or it is not effective to those not named. See Danyew v. Phelps, 676 P. 2d 707 (1983).

28 § 13-40-104(d) C.R.S., See also Tumbarello v. Byers, 543 P. 2d 1278 (Colo. 1975). If notice does not demand payment of rent or possession in alternative, it is defective.

29 § 13-40-104(e) C.R.S.

30 § 13-40-106 C.R.S., See Danyew v. Phelps, supra.

31 § 13-40-106 C.R.S.

32 § 13-40-106 C.R.S.; See also Hix v. Roy, 340 P. 2d 438 (Colo. 1959). Six month demand defective, failed to unequivocally terminate lease.

33 § 13-40-106; C.R.S. See also Hix v. Roy, 340 P. 2d at 440. All joint owners must sign demand. "One tenant in common cannot give notice for all without consent". But cf Didamo v. Tyrol Sport Arms Co. 680 P. 2d 1328, 1330 (Colo. 1984).

34 Hix v. Roy, 340 P. 2d 438 (Colo. 1959).

35 § 13-40-108 C.R.S.

36 Magliocco v. Olson, 762 P. 2d 681 (Colo. 1987).

37 § 13-40-108 C.R.S. See Danyew v. Phelps, 676 P. 2d 703 (Colo. 1983).

38 § 13-40-108; C.R.S.; e.g., service on visiting aunt would not be adequate.

39 § 13-40-108 C.R.S. See Magliocco v. Olson, 762 P. 2d 681 (Colo. 1987). Holding that notice by posting is adequate even if tenant does not see notice. Rubin, supra, Note 5 at 72; Koenigs, supra, Note 1 at 252; C. Krendl, *Colorado Methods of Practice,* West Vol. 2A § 2209 (1991) (hereinafter "Krendl").

40 Rubin, supra, Note 5 at 72; Koenigs, supra, Note 2 at 252; C. Krendl, *Colorado Methods of Practice,* West Vol. 2A § 2209 (1991) .

41 This would comport with the requirement of C.R.C.P. 4 (d). It is implicit in this rule that those over eighteen are more responsible and credible.

42 Rubin, supra, Note 5 at 252; C.R.C.P. 6(a); C.R.C.P. 306(a).

43 § 13-40-104(1)(e.5) C.R.S.

44 § 13-40-104(1)(e.5) C.R.S.; 13-40-106 C.R.S.; 13-40-107 C.R.S.

45 § 13-40-107.5 C.R.S.

46 § 13-40-107.5(3)(a) & (3)(b) C.R.S.

47 § 13-40-107.5(5)(a) C.R.S.

48 § 13-40-107.5(5)(b)(I) C.R.S.

49 § 13-40-107.5(5)(b)(II) C.R.S.

50 § 13-40-107 (4) C.R.S.; Didamo v. Tyrol Sport Arms Co., 680 P. 2d 1328 (Colo. 1984); July Building Corp. v. Heathrow & Co., Ltd., 679 P. 2d 1120 (Colo. 1984). Krendl, supra, Note 38 at § 2202 (See also additional cases cited therein).

51 Sinclair Refinery Co. v. Shakespeare, 175 P. 2d 387 (Colo. 1946), F. Anes: "Holdover Tenants in Colorado," 34 Rocky Mountain Law Review 320 (1962) (hereinafter "Anes"). This article contains a much more in-depth discussion of the subject.

52 Typically, language might be: "If after the expiration of this lease, the tenant, with the permission of the landlord, shall remain in possession of said premises...Tenant shall be regarded as a tenant from month-to-month..." See Apartment Lease No. 1045; Bradford Publishing Co.

53 Anes, supra at Note 51 at 324.

54 The Notice to Vacate is also known as "Notice to Quit" and informally called a "10 Day Notice" because the ten day notice period is the most common period required. This text will refer to this document as the Notice to Vacate because that is what the form is captioned.

55 § 13-40-107(1)(a), (c), (d) C.R.S.

56 § 13-40-107(1) C.R.S. (emphasis added.)

57 § 13-40-107 C.R.S.

58 C.R.C.P. 6(a); C.R.C.P. 306(a)

59 § 13-40-110 C.R.S.

60 C.R.C.P. 10, 310(a)

61 § 13-40-110 C.R.S.; See Kloepfer v. Keller, 1 Colo. 410 (Colo. 1871). Substantial facts must be set forth.

62 C.R.C.P. Rule 310, Doss v. Craig, 1 Colo. 177 (Colo. 1869)

63 If an attorney files the complaint, the verification is not necessary. C.R.C.P. 311. However, it is advisable to have same verified because it will aid you if a default judgment is sought. Koenigs, supra, Note 1 at 253.

64 C.R.C.P. 38, 338

65 § 13-40-111 C.R.S., C.R.C.P. 4, 304

66 §§ 13-40-111 C.R.S.; 13-40-112. This is a requirement under the due process clauses of the United States and Colorado Constitutions. It is taken very seriously by the courts and should be strictly complied with.

67 § 13-40-111 C.R.S.

68 C.R.C.P. 304; §13-40-111 C.R.S.

69 C.R.C.P. 4; C.R.C.P. 304

70 C.R.C.P. 304; C.R.C.P. 4.

71 § 13-40-109 C.R.S.

72 C.R.C.P. 4 (e); C.R.C.P. 304(d)

73 § 13-40-112 C.R.S.

74 § 13-40-112 C.R.S. It is advisable that a copy of the complaint also be mailed at that time. Mailing in addition to posting constitutes "due process" requirement, Greene v. Lindsey, 456 U.S. 444 (1982). Do not use certified mail, use regular first class mail, Krendl, supra, Note 39 at § 2221, fn 2. See also Dodge v. Meyer, 793 P. 2d 639 (Colo. 1990).

75 The requirement of mailing immediately after filing the complaint, before the plaintiff even knows if the defendant, after diligent attempts, may be served personally or by posting, is problematic. Unlike other civil actions in which an attorney may first issue and serve summons, and then file a complaint (See C.R.C.P. 3; C.R.C.P. 303), the statute appears clear that the summons may only be issued "upon filing the complaint ..." (See § 13-40-111 C.R.S.) Thus, under a strict reading of the statute, the plaintiff is required to mail the notice the day after filing the complaint, thus allowing for only one day of "diligent effort."

76 § 13-40-115 C.R.S. Typically, an "alias" summons will be issued for personal service upon the defendant as the case may be continued until the defendant is served. At that point, the court will consider economic claims.

77 C.R.C.P. 304(h)

78 See Magliocco v. Olson, 762 P. 2d 681 (Colo. App. 1987).

79 Continuing liability for subsequent rent after vacating solely depends on the language of the lease. Read it carefully. McArthur v. Rostek, 483 P. 2d 1351 (Colo. 1971) See Robert A. McNeil Corp. v. Paul, 757 P. 2d 165 (Colo. 1988); First National bank of Boston v. Dykstra, 684 P. 2d 957 (Colo. App. 1984); Emrich v. Joyce's Submarine Sandwiches, 751 P. 2d 651 (Colo. App. 1987). (All holding tenant liable) cf Aignor v. Cowell Sales Co., 660 P. 2d 907 (Colo. 1983) (Tenant not liable); See also Koenigs, supra, Note 1 at fn 7.

80 Additionally, the offer to cure must be unconditional. See Duran v. Housing Authority, 761 P. 2d 180 (Colo. 1988).

81 § 13-40-112 C.R.S., § 13-40-113 C.R.S.

82 § 13-40-113 C.R.S. Note that the appearance or filing of Answer will waive defective process defense.

83 C.R.C.P. County Court Form No. 3; C.R.C.P. District Court Form No. 17. With minor modification, the forms presented in this book will be acceptable for District Court.

84 Spar Consol. Mining & Development Co. v. Aasgaard, 516 P. 2d 127 (Colo. 1973)

85 Bonnell v. Gill, 92 P. 13 (Colo. 1907); McCrimmon v. Raymond, 234 P. 1058 (Colo. 1925)

86 § 13-40-113 C.R.S.; C.R.C.P. 312. Any defense not included in the answer is deemed waived (except subject matter jurisdiction). Id.

87 For additional information on defenses, see Ramos, supra, at Note 5. All defenses, other than defective notice, are applicable only to default evictions (as opposed to termination of tenancy situation).

88 Barlow v. Hoffman, 86 P. 2d 239 (Colo. 1938), Aigner v. Cowell Sales Co., 660 P. 2d 907 (Colo. 1983), Duran v. Housing Authority of City and County of Denver, 761 P. 2d 180 (Colo. 1988)

89 See Cypser "Survey of Colorado Landlord and Tenant Law," 20 Colo. Law 2023 (Colo. 1991). Of course, this is not applicable to termination of tenancy situation.

90 Werner v. Baker, 693 P.2d 385 (Colo. 1984); It should be noted that even if a lease requires that all modifications be in writing, this requirement too may be waived orally or by conduct. Williams v. Colo. Springs College of Business, 736 P. 2d 419 (Colo. 1987)

91 See Ramos, supra, Note 5 at 38-40.

92 Williams v. Colorado Springs College of Business, 736 P. 2d 419 (Colo. App. 1987)

93 Blazis v. Orlinski, 738 P. 2d 62, (Colo. App. 1987); Zarlengo v. Farrer, 683 P. 2d 1208 (Colo. App. 1984).

94 § 13-40-106, 13-40-107 C.R.S. See supra, Chapters IV and V. See also Audobon Commercial Area Co. v. Skelly Oil Co., 268 F. Supp. 883 (D. Colo. 1967).

95 § 13-40-104; 13-40-107 C.R.S.

96 Danyew v. Phelps, 676 P. 2d 707 (Colo. App. 1983)

97 § 13-40-104(1) C.R.S.; Ramos supra, at Note 5 at 7, 8

98 Tumbarello v. Byers, 543 P. 2d 1278 (Colo. App. 1975)

99 Rubin, supra, Note 5 at 70; Ramos, supra, Note 5 at 8.

100 See Ramos, supra, Note 5 at 28; interpreting Kirkland v. Allen, 678 P. 2d 568 (Colo. App. 1984) as implying that the landlord's breach occurring before a tenant's refusal to pay rent relieves the tenant from the duty to pay rent.

101 The extent of the disturbance must be relatively extreme so that a reasonable person would deem the premises as unusable. See e.g. Radinsky v. Weaver, supra (Landlord's construction on a second story caused water and dust to fall on expensive printing equipment, hole in roof of darkroom); Eskanos and Supperstein v. Irwin, supra (Loud music [including opera] from three different sources, simultaneously at tenant's quiet photo studio, in violation of specific lease provisions).

102 Candell v. Western Federal Savings and Loan Assn. of Denver, 400 P. 2d 909 (Colo. 1965); What a reasonable time is depends on the facts. See e.g., H&K Automotive Supply Co. v. Moore & Company, 657 P. 2d 986 (Colo. App. 1982) (Three years "unreasonable as a matter of law"); Eskanos, supra, (Tenant stayed on after making complaints "in good faith effort to work out solution" then left; this is reasonable). See also J.C. Penney & Co. v. Birrell, 32 P. 2d 805 (Colo. 1934) (What constitutes a reasonable time is a factual determination).

103 Isbill Associates v. City and County of Denver, 666 P. 2d 1117 (Colo. App. 1983); Kirkland v. Allen, 678 P. 2d 568 (Colo. App. 1984); Bedell v. Los Zapatistas, 805 P. 2d 1198 (Colo. 1991). See also Cypser supra, Note 5 at 2024. (But note that lack of abandonment does not allow for a constructive eviction claim as stated in Cypser's article.)

104 Radinsky v. Weaver, supra. Most leases do not waive a right to quiet enjoyment, but one should check the particular lease.

105 Shanahan v. Collins, 539 P. 2d 1261 (Colo. 1975) (Covenants dependent, defense allowed); GTM Investments v. The Depot, 694 P. 2d 379 (Colo. App. 1984) (Covenants independent, defense not allowed).

106 See Ramos, supra, Note 5 at 28. Forty-three other states have adopted the doctrine.

107 Blackwell v. Del Bosco, 558 P. 2d 563 (Colo. 1977); Bedell v. Los Zapatistas, 805 P. 2d 1198 (Colo. App. 1991). But see Chapter XII infra, regarding hazardous gas appliances.

108 Grolier Society v. International Realty Company, 482 P. 2d 394 (Colo. 1971); Aigner v. Cowell Sales Co., 660 P. 2d 407 (Colo. 1983); Robert McNeil Corporation v. Paul, 757 P. 2d 165 (Colo. App. 1968); Emrich v. Joyces Submarine Sandwiches, 751 P. 2d 651 (Colo. App. 1987); GTM Investments v. The Depot, 694 P. 2d 379 (Colo. App. 1984).

109 Schneiker v. Gordon, 732 P. 2d 603 (Colo. 1987); La Casa Nino v. Plaza Esteban, 762 P. 2d 669 (Colo. 1988)

110 C.R.C.P. 313. Almost all counterclaims which a tenant would bring in an eviction action would be deemed compulsory (Claim arising out of same parties, events, transactions). This must be brought at the same time or it will be barred.

111 Bedell v. Los Zapatistas, supra, quoting from the Restatement (Second) of Property, the court stated: "If the tenant is entitled to an abatement of the rent, the rent is abated to the amount of that proportion of the rent which the fair rental value after the event giving the right to abate bears to the fair rental value before the event. Abatement is allowed until the default is eliminated or the lease terminates, whichever first occurs". 805 P. 2d at 1200.

112 McCrea & Co. Auctioneers v. Dwyer Auto Body, 799 P. 2d 394 (Colo. App. 1990); Cablevision of Breckenridge, Inc. v. Tannhauser Condominium Assn., 649 P. 2d 1093 (Colo. 1982).

113 Hurricane v. Kanover, Ltd. 651 P. 2d 1218 (Colo. 1982) Rugg v. McCarty, 476 P. 2d 753 (Colo. 1970); Danyew v. Phelps, 676 P. 2d 707 (Colo. App. 1983). These torts require some very extreme or outrageous wrongful conduct on the part of defendant. For example, in Danyew v. Phelps, an elderly lady was evicted without statutory notice while she was incapacitated in the hospital She was, in fact, forced to spend more time in the hospital because she was "extremely upset and weakened by the knowledge of the eviction".

114 With minor modifications, these forms would be acceptable for district court. See C.R.C.P. Rules 8, 10, 12 and 13; and C.R.C.P. district court Form No. 17.

115 § 13-40-113 C.R.S.

116 If party files pro-se, C.R.C.P. 311

117 X v. Raymond, 234 P. 1058 (Colo. 1925), Bonnell v. Gill, 92 P. 13 (Colo. 1907); Spar Consol Mining and Development Co. v. Aasguard, 33 516 P. 2d 127 (Colo. App. 1973)

118 § 13-40-113 C.R.S.

119 C.R.C.P. 5; 305.

120 C.R.C.P. 38, 338. A jury trial makes the presentation of a case much more complex. If a jury is desired, a party would do well to retain an experienced trial attorney for the hearing.

121 Butler v. Farner, 704 P. 2d 853 (Colo. 1985)

122 § 13-40-114 C.R.S. Some commentators have construed § 13-40-114 C.R.S. as requiring trial within five days, however, cases and practice do not bear this out. There may be some court dockets which will not allow a trial to occur until longer than five days and there is no prohibition against a longer length. See Rubin, supra, Note 5 at 71 cf Ramos, supra Note 5 at 14; Cypser, supra, Note 5 at 226.

123 § 13-40-114 C.R.S.; Koenigs, supra, Note 1 at 253. Ramos, supra, Note 5 at 14. Ramos points out that this requirement is misread by many courts.

124 C.R.C.P. 355. Note that if the defendant was not personally served (i.e., served by posting) the court only has jurisdiction to enter an order for possession and not monetary damages; C.R.C.P. 13-40-115.

125 C.R.C.P. 307(b); 312(b). Certain exceptions exist to this rule but should not be of concern in the typical eviction.

126 The procedure for default judgment in district court is somewhat different. See C.R.C.P. 55; if in district court, be sure to comply with C.R.C.P. 121, § 1-14 which requires that a number of specific documents be prepared.

127 § 13-40-112 C.R.S. An alias summons may be issued and the court may continue the case for purpose of establishing monetary damages. § 13-40-115 C.R.S.

128 C.R.C.P. 355

129 David R. DeMuro, *Colorado Civil Trial Practice,* (1986) § 384 (here inafter "DeMuro"). See e.g., C.R.C.P. Chapter 33 (Rules of Evidence).

130 Jack Friedenthal et al., *Civil Procedure,* (1985) § 10.1 (hereinafter "Friedenthal"); DeMuro, supra, Note 105 at § 384; Thomas Mauet, *Fundamentals of Trial Techniques,* (2d ed. 1988) pp. 1-21 (hereinafter "Mauet").

131 See generally, Mauet, supra, Note 105 at 45-74.

132 See C.R.C.P. 343(f). If original documents are unavailable, additional proof surrounding reason for unavailability must be presented.

133 C.R.C.P. 343; Colorado Rules of Evidence ("C.R.E.") 101 et seq..

134 C.R.E. 401

135 C.R.E. 602, 801-803

136 C.R.C.P. 343; C.R.E. 1002, 1003

137 C.R.E. 901, 902

138 See C.R.E. 101 et seq.. The rules of evidence are extremely complex and this discussion does not even scratch the surface.

139 C.R.C.P. 41, § 13-40-116, C.R.S. This is applicable to counterclaims by defendant. See also C.R.C.P. 350 regarding County Court motions for directed verdict.

140 C.R.C.P. 41, 341. If defendant is successful, he may recover against plaintiff for his costs. § 13-40-110, C.R.S.

141 C.R.C.P. 352 (Note, this applies to non-jury county court cases only). However, in "exceptional" cases, the court may take cases under advisement.

142 § 13-40-115(2), § 13-40-123 C.R.S.; C.R.C.P. 354(d)

143 § 13-40-115(2), § 13-40-123 C.R.S.; See also Magliocco v. Olson, 762 P. 2d 681 (Colo. 1987); Del E. Webb Realty and Management Co. v. Wessbecker, 628 P. 2d 114 (Colo. App. 1981); Collins v. Shanahan, 523 P. 2d 999 (Colo. App. 1974), affd. 539 P. 2d 1261 (Colo. 1976). It should be noted that although the statute provides for recovery of attorneys' fees in practice, judges have seemed to be unwilling to enforce these provisions or will unilaterally reduce the claimed fees. See Ramos, supra, Note 5 at 17; Krendl, supra, Note 39 at § 2226.

144 § 13-40-122 C.R.S.

145 See e.g., § 13-40-117, 118, 120, 121 C.R.S.; C.R.C.P. 411, County Court Forms 4 and 5.

146 § 13-40-118, 120 C.R.S. These payments may be distributed to landlord upon order of court. § 13-40-121 C.R.S. If the defendant fails to pay any of these, the appeal will be dismissed. §§ 13-40-118, 120 C.R.S.

147 § 13-40-117(3) C.R.S. For a further discussion of appeal requirements, see Ramos, supra, Note 5 at 18-20; Krendl, supra, Note 39 at § 2225.

148 § 38-12-103(1) C.R.S. Note that there may exist local ordinances also requiring payment of interest upon security deposits. However, no state law exists.

149 § 38-12-103(1) C.R.S.

150 § 38-12-103(1)C.R.S.; Chew v. International Society for Krishna Consciousness of Colorado, 738 P. 2d 57 (Colo. App. 1987) (Ordinary wear and tear defined). "'Normal wear and tear' means that deterioration which occurs based upon the use for which the rental unit is intended, without negligence, carelessness, accident or abuse of the premises or equipment or chattels by the tenant, or members of his household or their invitees, members or their guests". § 38-12-102(1) C.R.S.

151 It is doubtful that a security deposit claim would exceed $10,000.00. But, if it does, it must be filed in the District Court.

152 See generally, § 13-6-401 et seq. C.R.S.; C.R.C.P. 501 et seq.

153 § 13-6-404 and 407 C.R.S. Note, however, that an attorney may appear to represent himself or herself and if an attorney so appears, the opposing party may be represented by counsel. § 13-6-404(2)(4) C.R.S.

154 Guzman v. McDonald, 570 P. 2d 532 (Colo. 1977) (More specifically "(1) wilful retention and (2) wrongful detention"); See also Martinez v. Steinbaum, 623 P. 29 49 (Colo. 1981).

155 Turner v. Lyon, 539 P. 2d 1241 (Colo. 1975)

156 Heatherridge Management Company v. Benson, 558 P. 2d 435 (Colo. 1977)

157 § 38-12-104 C.R.S.

Bibliography

Note: *Colo. Law* is an abbreviation for *The Colorado Lawyer Magazine* published monthly, and available from the Colorado Bar Association (1-800-332-6736).

F. Anes, "Holdover Tenants in Colorado," 34 *Rocky Mountain Law Review* 320 (1962). In-depth discussion of holdover tenancy and termination thereof.

D. Cypser, "Survey of Colorado Landlord Tenant Law," 20 *Colo. Law* 2023 (Oct. 1991). Contains discussions of many recent cases and statutes regarding all aspects of landlord/tenant relations. Especially good discussion on self-help and landlord's liens.

J. Gigax, "Rights of Landlords in Tenant's Personal Property," 57 *Denv. U.L.J.* 685 (1980). In-depth discussion of landlord's liens.

C. Koenigs, "Enforcement of Leases Through Unlawful Detainer Actions," 20 *Colo. Law* 251 (Feb. 1991). This article contains a good, but brief, overview of the eviction process. Good "common sense" suggestions.

Cathleen Krendl, *Colorado Methods of Practice, Volume 2A,* West (1991). The standard's basic reference text among Colorado attorneys. Covers a wide variety of subjects. Chapter on eviction covers major steps. It is directed at attorneys already familiar with basic civil procedure.

Manuel A. Ramos, *Rights and Obligations: Colorado Landlord-Tenant Law From the Perspective of a Tenant Advocate,* (1992) (Published by and available through Continuing Legal Education of Colorado, Inc., Phone: 303-860-0608). Everything you ever wanted to know about tenant rights. Written in the style of a legal brief, filled with comprehensive information with citations to cases. May be too technical for the layman.

M. Ramos, "Colorado's Landlord Lien Statute: Equal Protection and Due Process Infirmities," 11 *Colo. Law* 1867 (July 1982). Tenant's rights advocate view of landlord's lien statute. Constitutional law perspective.

D. Rubin, "Representation of the Landlord in an Unlawful Detainer Action," 12 *Colo. Law* 69 (Oct. 1973). Landlord's perspective on evictions. Suggestion to protect landlord and attorney representing landlord from liability.

Index

Order Form

Other Titles Available From Bradford Publishing

- Friendly Divorce Guidebook for Colorado $32.95
- Vehicles and Traffic, Title 42, C.R.S. 9.50
- Colorado Court Rules 24.50
- Wills, Trust and Estate Planning (Attorney Handbook) 27.50
- Attorney's Handbook on Consumer Bankruptcy and Chapter 13 .... 23.95

☐ Please send me a catalog of all Bradford Publishing Legal Forms, Books and Supplies.

☐ Please notify me of updates to this book.

All forms shown in this book are available at Bradford Publishing Company. For prices, quantity discounts and ordering information, please call us.

Title	Price	Quantity	Total
		Subtotal	
		Postage ($3.50 for 1 book; plus .75 each additional	
		Subtotal	
		Tax: Denver – 7.3%; CO 3% Denver Metro RTD 3.8%	
		Total	

Method of Payment:

☐ Check or Money Order

☐ VISA ☐ MasterCard

Account No. ______________________________ Exp. __________

Name ____________________ Signature ____________________

Street Address ____

City ____________________ State __________ Zip __________

Send or Fax to: **BRADFORD PUBLISHING CO.**

1743 Wazee Street • Denver, Colorado 80202

Mail Order (303) 292-2590 • Fax (303) 298-5014